"It's a very inviting book for anyone who is ready to change their lifestyle."
~ Nicole Duval, Oshawa,

"'Be The Change' is an ex<
on and see how the autho
From what I was able to r

. The author clearly has a talent and desire to help people find a path to better themselves and the world around them. I am so thankful for the wonderful things this book will bring each person who reads it."
~ Jessica, Rochester, NY, United States of America

"The author has put a lot of effort and resources into this book. I can tell she has done her homework."
~ Gabriel Robitaille, Private Address

"It is so easy to use this book all year long for recipes and guidance. I can't wait to have a hard copy that I can keep it handy through the seasons and ensure I continue to make positive changes for each moon cycle and embrace the changes. The author's message is clear and the information flows perfectly. I love how inspiring the book is. Just like the author, it is going to be a positive influence in the lives of anyone it touches. I am so happy I got to read it already! I've identified three rituals I want to incorporate this year and three habits I want to eliminate and I'm getting into gear for a vision board!! This book is super informative and inspiring and interactive. Anyone who is looking for self help books and growth will love it and there's definitely useful information for any type of reader!!"
~ Chantelle, F, Muskoka, ON, Canada

"A lot of the concerns I had about my health were all discussed fully and it only brighten me to look deeper into a healthier lifestyle. I hope there will be a second book and many more to come from you Ashley!"
~ Janelle, Newmarket, ON, Canada

Be The Change

Your Guide to Elemental Growth Through Nature, Love, Food, and Movement

By

ASHLEY MICHAUD | INHC, HHC

Be The Change: Your Guide to Elemental Growth Through Nature, Love, Food, and Movement

© Ashley Michaud | INHC, HHC © 2019 Elemental Growth.

All Rights Reserved. No part of this book can be scanned, distributed or copied without permission. This book or any portion thereof may not be reproduced or used in any manner whatsoever without the express written permission of the author and publisher at ashley@elementalgrowth.org - except for the use of brief quotations in a book review.

The author has independently contributed to the content of this book and has made every effort to ensure the accuracy of the information within this book was correct at time of publication. The author does not assume and hereby disclaims any liability to any party for any loss, damage, or disruption caused by errors or omissions, whether such errors or omissions result from accident, negligence, or any other cause. This book is not intended to be a substitute for the medical advice of a licensed physician. The reader should consult with their doctor in any matters relating to his / her health.

The publisher is not responsible for websites (or their content) that are not owned by the publisher.

Published by:
Ashley Michaud
Elemental Growth Org.
307-280 Wentworth Street,
Oshawa, Ontario,
Canada, L1J 1N2

Editing & Interior Book Design: Warrior Life Creative Co.
Cover Design: Ashley Michaud

A CIP record for this book is available from the Library of Congress Cataloging-in-Publication Data

ISBN-13: 978 1097586912

Printed in Canada

Dedication

I have written this book for those . . .

Who are ready for something better
than who they were in the past!

The open-minded who showed me love, encouraged
my personal growth, and continue to stand by
me as we ride this roller coaster called life.

Last in my book but first in my heart, I am dedicating this
work to my son, Fynn Oliver Michaud, it's all happening!

Contents

PREFACE	13
INTRODUCTION - BE THE CHANGE	15
THE ELEMENTAL GROWTH PROTOCOL	23
CHAPTER 1 - WINTER RESOLUTIONS (EARTH)	27
INTRODUCTION	28
WINTER SOLSTICE	29
MOON CYCLES	30
CIRCADIAN RHYTHM	32
WINTER FOOD GUIDE	33
WINTER RECIPES	34
MOVEMENT	41
CHECK-IN ACTIVITIES	43
CHAPTER 2 - SPRING CLEAN (WATER)	47
INTRODUCTION	48
SPRING EQUINOX	49
MOON CYCLES	50
CIRCADIAN RHYTHM	52
SPRING FOOD GUIDE	53
SPRING RECIPES	54

MOVEMENT	64
CHECK-IN ACTIVITIES	66

CHAPTER 3 - SUMMER LOVE (FIRE) — 69

INTRODUCTION	70
SUMMER SOLSTICE	71
MOON CYCLES	72
CIRCADIAN RHYTHM	74
SUMMER FOOD GUIDE	75
SUMMER RECIPES	76
MOVEMENT	86
CHECK-IN ACTIVITIES	87

CHAPTER 4 - FALL ELIMINATION (AIR) — 91

INTRODUCTION	92
FALL EQUINOX	93
MOON CYCLES	95
CIRCADIAN RHYTHM	96
FALL FOOD GUIDE	98
FALL RECIPES	99
MOVEMENT	108
CHECK-IN ACTIVITIES	109

CHAPTER 5 - TRUE ALCHEMY (AETHER) — 115

INTRODUCTION	116
CHAKRA MAPPING	117
CREATE YOUR OWN TRADITIONS	121
MOON CYCLES AND REGULATING OUR HORMONE CYCLE	123

CIRCADIAN RHYTHM - MORNING ROUTINE CHECKLIST	127
ELEMENTAL RHYTHM - NIGHT ROUTINE CHECKLIST	128
FOOD GUIDE - EAT THE RAINBOW	129
BUILD YOUR MENU - EATING FOR YOUR CHAKRAS	131
PLAN YOUR MEALS - PLANNER & SHOPPING LIST	136
MOVEMENT - CREATE YOUR FITNESS STYLE	137
TRACK YOUR FITNESS	138
CHECK-IN ACTIVITIES	140
SACRED WORD OF EMPOWERMENT	143
RECIPE SHARE	144
WELLNESS TINCTURES & REMEDIES	149
FINAL THOUGHTS	**151**
ELEMENTAL GROWTH INDEX	**155**
ACKNOWLEDGMENT	**164**
ABOUT THE AUTHOR	**165**
JOURNAL	**168**

How To Use This Book

This book may be read once and passed on to someone else or read over and over, year after year, with new intentions and goals in mind.

Furthermore, you will find an opportunity to further develop these practices and make them your own—honor this process and trust that you already have all you need to heal and be your best self.

Be The Change is an interactive book with multiple avenues for support, guidance, coaching, and implementation. For example, you can become an Elemental Member, receive coaching support from me, access bonus content, or connect with the Elemental Growth community. Additionally, there is space for note taking, doodling, and writing messages to yourself / friends.

Looking for more seasonal recipes, more in depth information, or a friend to hold you accountable on your health and wellness journey, join our online community on Facebook and Instagram.

www.elementalgrowth.org
youtube: Elemental Growth
fb: @IamElementalGrowth | ig: @IamElementalGrowth

Preface

"Be the change you wish to see in the world."
— Mahatma Gandhi

After many years of contemplating my own life decisions, experiences, and journey, I realized one thing: If I was ever going to embrace the changes I needed to make for myself, I had to learn from the master of change herself—Mother Nature. I dove into the world of Consciousness Expanding Ceremony first, which ignited my childhood passion for foraging and herbology. Following this, I started practicing permaculture, Kundalini yoga, chakra therapies, and Reiki. To say I became obsessed with natural alternatives and healing techniques using nature, food, love, and movement would be an understatement.

    I took things a step further and began studying at the world's largest nutrition school, The Institute for Integrative Nutrition® (IIN). Today, I have been certified as a Reiki Master, an Integrative Nutrition Health Coach, a Hormone Health Coach, and a Coaching Master. During my time as a student, I developed four seasonal coaching groups:

ASHLEY MICHAUD

Winter Resolutions, Spring Clean, Summer Love, and Fall Elimination with the intent to connect and guide others who are ready to be the change we wish to see in the world.

These groups are all about change—becoming one with nature and her rhythms, embracing the natural cycles of change, finding your tribe, and transforming yourself. I launched my first group in Spring 2018, which inspired thirty individuals to embrace change, while creating and implementing the sustainable health and lifestyle changes they were seeking. I personally host one group coaching event each season for twenty-eight days so that our community can receive year round support from myself as well as each other. These groups are ever-changing just as we are. Some people join every season, while some pop in and out. The goal is to take each protocol and make it your own, so let's get started!

INTRODUCTION

Becoming The Change

ASHLEY MICHAUD

"The tiny seed knew that in order to grow, it needed to be dropped in dirt, covered in darkness, struggle to reach the light."
— *Sandra Kring*

Each of us has a story to tell, a voice that needs to be heard, and a soul that needs to be healed and soothed. Yet we often don't tune into these needs unless we are at a point of no return; a point where we can choose to embrace change in all its glory – see what lies ahead and grow with it or stay stagnant in our current circumstances. Since you are reading this book, it is safe to assume that you have arrived at your turning point—a time where you are ready to dig deep, turn within, and embrace change and healing in all its forms. Like you, I too, was at a similar crossroads, and this is why, out of all the topics I could write about, I chose to write about Mother Nature and her cyclical seasons. After all, who in this world embraces change better than Mother Nature herself?

   Embracing nature's seasonal messages helped me get more attuned with myself—my heart, my body, my spirit. Paying attention to how everything is interconnected and woven through nature's cycles has positively affected my health and happiness every step of the way. Embracing Mother Nature's cyclical seasonal guidance gave me the strength and tools I needed to overcome my family karma: a bloodline of addiction, abuse, mental, and hormonal imbalances. Moon cycles are a part of this seasonal guidance—tuning into the moon cycles made change enjoyable, trackable, and held me accountable for each action step and goal I set for myself.

I tracked my activities, progress, and failures which enabled me to achieve my goals at an exponential rate. This has now evolved into a full swing holistic practice where I facilitate, lead, and coach others on the Elemental Growth protocol and how to live in sync with the seasons. These groups continue to grow and inspire others to turn their pain into power, passion into action, and goals into realities.

As creatures of habit and comfort, we steer away from the unknown, the uncomfortable, the unexplainable. We fear change because we fear what we have never experienced. However, the truth is that life is all about experience, and as you read this book, you will discover my signature protocol to embrace change and enjoy the experience that is Elemental Growth to craft your own healing experience.

ALL WE HAVE IS CHANGE

Nature is ever changing, and yet it is cyclical with developed cycles that encourage elemental growth for both the individual and the collective. Take a moment to check-in with yourself about your cycles:

Is there a pattern or cycle you keep repeating?
Do your daily rituals align with your goals?
What would you like to change in your life?

_____
_____
_____

I spent a lot of my time outdoors and I moved around frequently in my life. Through these experiences, I noticed many of nature's secret messages. I was curious about how the moon looked different each night and how there were different moon cycles each month. I noticed that the seasons each contained thirteen weeks and three moon cycles of approximately twenty-eight days each. I noted seasonal foods and developed the skills of foraging, wildcrafting, and herbology.

I realized at a young age that change was not something to fear, in fact, there is a comfort in change—there is comfort in knowing you are alive, growing, and thriving. I love how simple life became for me once I tuned into nature's cycles to embody and become the change I wished to see and experience in the world.

Yes, change is scary, but it's constant. In fact, it may be the only constant we have. Although it can be nerve-wracking to completely surrender, imagine if we reframed that feeling and thought to one of ease, effortlessness, and growth? What if we focused on how surrendering could be easy and even benefit us in ways we never imagined?

I AM ELEMENTAL GROWTH

My story begins in a confusing, dark, and lonely world as I watched unhealthy lifestyle choices create a ripple effect of ill health in my world—mentally, physically, and emotionally. Alcohol, opioids, abuse, and sad lifestyle choices rippled through my bloodline and relationships. Were we all victims? Was this how it is going to be? Was this all there was to my life?

By the time I was fourteen years old, I had moved away from home and was living on my own. In my fourteen years at home, I had experienced parental abandonment along with sexual, physical, and mental abuse by the very people who were supposed to guide me and protect me. The worst part in all of this was that I was heading down a dark path myself.

I began smoking cigarettes at the tender age of nine, followed by alcohol consumption shortly after. By the time I was in high school, I was selling and actively using ecstasy on a daily basis, not to mention putting myself in some very scary and provocative situations. I did not value life at all and attempted suicide on three different occasions during my high school years despite having a strong group of girlfriends and elders who believed I could do better than my parents.

When I turned seventeen, my dad passed away (R.I.P) from a morphine overdose. When I was twenty-one, prescription drugs and poor lifestyle choices had fully taken over my mom's life as well. My mom had a severe overdose from Fentanyl and I was the one who had to witness that and ultimately make the decision to save her life. Despite my feelings of anger towards her and fear of losing the only parent I had at the time, my mom survived and became motivated to ditch all prescription drugs for good this time.

I spent many years after that fateful day traveling across Canada, working wherever I lived and honing the skills and lifestyle of a hospitality and tourism student. For a decade, I moved across the country working in bars, golf courses, healthy restaurants, chain restaurants, hotels, and even direct sales for companies such as Labatte and Diageo.

At work, I was focused, driven, goal oriented, always working to the best of my ability. However, when I didn't work, I partied, and whenever I drank and the party ended, my past trauma would come rushing back to me. I'd remember all the hurtful, scary, and sad memories. However, when I worked, I served a purpose and my past memories would be a distant thought, if that. I made friends quickly, talked people through their problems, and I was always seen as the fun, wild, and positive girl, ready to help anyone.

In 2014, I chose to return to the area I grew up in. I was going through an awakening and realized that the life I was living was not for me. Things had to change—my daily activities did not align with my core values and in fact, enabled others to make unhealthy lifestyle choices as well. I knew better. I knew I was better and I knew that I could better serve others by developing the skills I am passionate about and aligning my lifestyle with my contemplated values.

All change starts within and needs to start with oneself, so I knew in order to start this journey of change and Elemental Growth, I needed to come back to my roots, my family, and the place where it all happened. When I returned, the first thing I eliminated was nicotine, followed by alcohol, and unhealthy food. From there, I made even more room for forgiveness, self-love, conscious awareness, and self-actualization which has brought me to where I am today. I am a mother, guide, author, and lover of life!

In 2014, I began practicing Kundalini yoga and learning about the chakra system. In 2015, my journey lead me through Columbia, Ecuador, and Peru where I learned how to love myself and nurture my intuition. In 2016, I gave birth to my son at home, naturally, without any intervention; A child, the doctors said I likely could not conceive or carry to term due to hormonal and cervical complications. Later that same year, I was attuned as a Reiki Master.

In 2017, I started my herbology and Reiki practice and in 2018, I graduated from the Institute for Integrative Nutrition (IIN) where I was trained by the top experts in

Be The Change

the world on nutrition and lifestyle. I graduated at the top of my class and today, I guide others to transform their addictive behavior into alchemy.

I am grateful every day for the new foundation I have built—for my friends, mentors, and teachers who encouraged me to believe in something better for myself. But ultimately it is my willpower that transformed my passion into action, it is me who created this life, it is me who took each step, and it is me who can guide you to tap into your passion and begin your own Elemental Growth journey with community and tons of tools that I have adapted through my experience and diverse training.

You don't have to go on this journey alone, in fact, having your own personal coach will only serve you. I provide you everything you need to align your natural rhythm, activate your body's natural healing processes, and help you rise up and step into your true potential.

Like me, you already have everything you need to heal and live your dreams. The question is: *Are you ready to make it happen?*

List 1-3 things that you are ready to release followed by 1-3 things you want to see manifest in your future. You will be surprised how powerful these simple bio-hacking activities can be!

_____

_____

_____

_____

_____

The Elemental Growth Protocol

"Through the ever changing seasons of life, know that you have it within you to find your way back to yourself."
– Tania Jane Moraes-Vaz

There are many protocols out there and many ways to embrace nature but what's unique about this one is every tool is available to you when, where, and how you need it. The more aligned with nature you are, the more you will be in the right place, at the right time, for the right reason.

WHAT YOU NEED TO KNOW

- **Elements:** Earth (my Body), Air (my Breath), Fire (my Spirit), Water (my Flow)
- **Equinox / Solstice**: Track your success(es), celebrate holidays, and celebrate yourself
- **Full Moon:** Release what no longer serves you, detox your mind, body, soul, and environment, cleansing and clearing, outgoing, sexually motivated
- **New Moon:** Ask and manifest, introverted, dreamer, inner work
- **Circadian Rhythm:** Rise and set with the sun, optimize your health and mood
- **Seasonal Food Guides:** Enhance your health with these eco-thrifty hacks
- **Movement:** Release your pain, thoughts, emotions– Free your soul
- **Check-in Activities:** Practice self-love with these guided exercises

SEASONAL COACHING

Each program runs for the length of each season. This means you will receive support and guidance year round with a different focus every three months to better align you with nature and each season's unique messages.

WINTER RESOLUTIONS

Opens in January - The group for planting seeds, germinating thoughts, feelings, and beliefs that will grow as you do. It is time to renew your values so that you can change transform and create the reality you desire.

SPRING CLEAN

Opens in April - The group that encourages you to follow your heart and take action on your ideas. The warmth brings wisdom and brings forth directions from your soul so you can tune in and more easily recognize them.

SUMMER LOVE

Opens in July - The group that enables you to awaken your energetic body and open the channels to your Higher Self. This is an excellent time to try something new that will challenge you and energize your body, mind, and spirit.

FALL ELIMINATION

Opens in October - The group that brings awareness to where you are now. This is a time to set goals for the year ahead, make changes, focus on your higher purpose, and do the work necessary so your goals become your reality.

THINGS MY CLIENTS SAY

"I learned a lot about healthy alternatives and how to make meals more nutritious. Now that I know it's so much easier to eat healthy."

"I felt very supported and feel like it strengthened my friendships even more."

"Ashley is friendly and the results are always of the highest quality. I'm looking forward to continuing on."

"I updated some of my goals that I had identified at the beginning, then as we went on I achieved others."

"This program brings efficiency to a new level. Ashley keeps things simple and informative which helped me to lose weight, cook healthy foods at home, and love exercise."

"It has been empowering to learn about what I'm putting in my body. I am also better at protecting myself, setting boundaries, and giving myself permission to put myself first. Ashley offers gentle guidance and loving support emotionally, spiritually and physically."

"I got so much more than I ever expected. I make better food choices now, and my kitchen is stocked with more nutritious food. I feel more balanced, I am sleeping better, I have more energy and open to new things."

CHAPTER 1
Winter Resolutions (Earth)

ASHLEY MICHAUD

"Winter is a season of recovery and preparation."
— Paul Theroux

We have eyes to witness the process of change, a sense that each season sets the stage for the next, but oftentimes, we don't embrace these parts of ourselves fully, the way we are meant to. Each season has a unique message for every living creature in nature. Each season draws attention to our individual needs so we may grow and evolve as we are meant to. Winter is governed by the element of earth, it symbolizes our inner worldliness. Winter grounds us in reality so we can create the foundation we need to step into the life we desire.

Most of the year, we live in harmony with nature and witness its beautiful elements and the changes that come with it. However during winter, we often have a tendency to completely disconnect from nature, especially in current society where we have an array of choices before us such as staying indoors and indulging in indoor activities versus venturing outdoors. We don't have to go outdoors if we don't want to and can stay up all hours of the night on our phone and Netflix regardless of how many hours of sunlight we get in a day.

On January 1st of each year, we celebrate the new year; we share our goals and intentions for the year ahead with excitement and enthusiasm. Some of the most common goals and resolutions are things such as quitting smoking, getting out of debt, starting a diet or fitness routine and finally "sticking" to it, but so often we fail within the first month. but so often we fail within the first month.

While I don't encourage you to view failure as a "bad" thing, it can be disappointing and sometimes cripple our growth.

In this chapter, I show you the Elemental Growth protocol for Winter Resolutions because I want to see you achieve your individual goals this year.

What are your intentions?

What changes do you want to make for your health, mindset, career, health, and environment?

What changes have you been craving—on an emotional, physical, spiritual level?

_____

_____

_____

_____

_____

WINTER SOLSTICE

Traditionally, winter solstice celebrated the rebirth of the Sun and longer days. People would keep a fire going for twelve days to light up the sun, each year's fire is lit with a log from the previous year - this is also known as a Yule log. Around the world, people share food, sing, dance, and play instruments to celebrate. Hot baths and yoga are also a tradition to many.

Today we celebrate Christmas with our loved ones, gifts and food. Then one week later, we celebrate the new year by staying up until midnight and setting our intentions for the year ahead. This may vary depending on cultural and individual traditions, so take a minute to think about your own traditions up to today.

- Where are these traditions rooted?
- Do these traditions serve you today?

_____
_____
_____
_____
_____

Nature teaches us how to take what works and build from there. Things in nature can seem complex but directly responsible for our activities. Nature's cycles present us with a process that enhances our Elemental Growth. Winter solstice is the perfect time for planting seeds, germinating thoughts, feelings, and beliefs that will grow as you do. It is time to renew your values so that you can change transform and create the reality you desire.

Think of 1-3 rituals that you will want to include next year, and contemplate 1-3 patterns, behaviors, habits, cycles that you want to release. Write these down in next year's calendar so you can track your goals and create your own tradition based on your unique beliefs and experiences.

MOON CYCLES

Get out your calendar and mark down each full and new moon for the year ahead (you can get your moon guide for free at www.elementalgrowth.org/promos). There are thirteen weeks, ninety-one days, and approximately three to four moon cycles each season. The simplified moon cycle is twenty-eight days, the same as our hormonal cycle.

In the Elemental Growth protocol, we focus on the full

moon and new moon. The full moon is a time to release old patterns, beliefs, and habits and cleanse ourselves and our environment. You will feel more outgoing and sexually motivated. The new moon is a time for asking and manifesting—a time where we can not only declare our intentions and desires but also begin taking the action steps to manifest them. We will feel more introverted and likely map out our dreams and do the inner work necessary for Elemental Growth.

NEW MOON

If you look up to the sky during a new moon, it will seem dark and empty. So often we feel that way ourselves during this time and are more likely to stay indoors. Even animals get mellow around this time of the month. Although you may notice that your senses and sensitivity are heightened during this phase. With a shift in perspective, you may realize that the dark sky is actually a blank canvas for us to create our month ahead.

FULL MOON

Animals get really active during a full moon. This time of year, they don't have a lot of energy so they conserve it for a time when they can be most productive. This means they are hunting, gathering, building, and mating under the full moon skies. We have these instincts too and by all means, I encourage you to embrace them. Use this as a time to go after the things you want, gather what you need for the weeks ahead, structure your goals in order of priority and break down your actions steps.

- **Full Wolf Moon:** In January, wolves begin to get particularly loud and vocal because mating season begins in February. For us however, it's a lesson to trust the messages that our instincts, heart, and mind are conveying to us. *How can you use this time to gain control over your life?*

- **Full Snow Moon:** Typically occurs in February, which is also when the heaviest snowfall takes place and hunting becomes very difficult. Many would live on bone broth and couldn't travel far from their home. Although we have snow plows, grocery stores, and heated vehicles today, it's still a good time to stay indoors and enjoy the ones you love.

- **Full Worm Moon:** In March, the ground begins to thaw and earthworms reappear, soon followed by robins—the first sign of spring. For some, this is a season of Lent, when you give something up for forty days and forty nights. A time to fast and reflect for spring is just around the corner.

CIRCADIAN RHYTHM

All living organisms on earth, ranging from fungi to plants and animals, even humans, have a circadian clock and operate on a circadian rhythm. A circadian rhythm is any biological process that repeats within about twenty-four hours. These twenty-four hour rhythms are driven by a circadian clock, they include hormone regulation, energy, and vibration, sleep, hunger, health, mood, and other daily functions too.

The amount of daylight we receive during the winter may vary depending on where you live. I am providing you a general guideline to optimize your daily routine and get the most out of yourself and your day. The goal during the winter season is to eat breakfast and do a quick exercise before sunrise, like HIIT or dancing to your favorite song, for a duration of five or ten minutes.

Take this a step further and plan your nighttime routine about two hours after supper. This will begin intermittent fasting which is helpful in regulating blood sugar and help you to create a healthy sleeping habit. Winter is a time for us to rest. It is Mother Nature's way of asking us to slow down, rejuvenate, and relax, so embrace it.

- **January:** Daylight between 8am and 5pm
- **February:** Daylight between 7:30am and 5:30pm
- **March:** Daylight between 7am and 6pm

FOOD GUIDE & RECIPES

Having spent the first quarter of my life in the hospitality industry followed by graduating from the world's largest nutrition school, and now as an established herbalist and plant-based alternatives expert, you can see how being a healthy foodie developed naturally.

Each season I will use this guide to show you a different method to connect with your food and understand the benefits of conscious eating. Your body has everything it needs to heal and run efficiently, but to optimize and supercharge your health and lifestyle you must fuel your flesh-vehicle with premium food.

During winter, I find myself focusing on micro and macro nutrient content which is what is included in your winter food guide as a general reference. I invite you to take this a step further and try a health and nutrition tracking app for a week or longer to measure your progress between where you start at today and where you want to be. My recommendations are My Fitness Pal FitBit, and Chronometer but there are many built-in Health apps available for all phone types, so pick one that resonates with you and commit to using it for a certain amount of time. Flip the page for some of our favorite winter foods and recipes for Elemental Growth along with some healing and nourishing remedies and tinctures. Enjoy!

ASHLEY MICHAUD

Breakfast - Spiced Pear Bake

INGREDIENTS

2 cups of oats
1 can coconut milk
2 tablespoons melted coconut oil
¼ cup maple syrup
1 teaspoon baking powder
1 teaspoon cinnamon
1 teaspoon ginger
1 teaspoon nutmeg
2 teaspoons vanilla extract
2-3 thinly sliced pears
½ cup chopped walnuts
Salt to taste

DIRECTIONS

- In a bowl, mix 2 cups of oats, 1 can coconut milk, 2 tablespoons melted coconut oil, ¼ cup maple syrup, 1 teaspoon baking powder, 1 teaspoon cinnamon, 1 teaspoon ginger, 1 teaspoon nutmeg, 2 teaspoons vanilla extract.
- Add to cast iron skillet or deep dish pie pan.
- Garnish with 2-3 thinly sliced pears, ½ cup chopped walnuts and a dash of salt.
- Bake at 350 degrees for 40 minutes.

AM Snack – Cinasim Smoothie

INGREDIENTS

1-2 persimmons
1 apple
1 Frozen banana
Cinnamon sticks (Feel free to use ground cinnamon powder)
Chia seeds or hemp seeds
Maca root (optional)
Plant-based milk (dairy-free)

DIRECTIONS

- Blend the persimmon(s), apple(s), frozen banana(s), cinnamon, chia/hemp seeds, and plant-based milk and maca root (optional).

- Enjoy cold or at room temperature.

ASHLEY MICHAUD

Lunch - Harvest Sandwich

INGREDIENTS

Crushed walnuts
2 slices of bread or 1 or 2 wholegrain wraps
Field greens
1 sliced pear
1 can of chickpeas
¼ cup tahini
Cumin powder
Salt to taste
Lemon to taste
Garlic to taste (2-3 cloves should be ideal.)

DIRECTIONS

HUMMUS

- Blend 1 can chickpeas, ¼ cup tahini, cumin, salt, garlic, and lemon to taste.

SANDWICH PREP

- Mix crushed walnuts with hummus and spread onto toast or wrap.
- Add field greens and sliced pear.
- Good on most bread, wraps or buns. We get the gluten-free and vegan bagels from O'doughs.

PM Snack - Rainbow Hash

INGREDIENTS
5-6 potatoes
1 head of cabbage
1 onion
1 broccoli head
Salt to taste
Dijon mustard to season and taste

DIRECTIONS
- Always cook potatoes in a batch the night before and chill to create resistant starch the kind that is low on the glycemic index.
- Cube or grate these potatoes, then fry them up with red cabbage, onions, broccoli, salt and Dijon mustard.

Supper – Loaded Miso Soup

INGREDIENTS

1 bag or box of mushrooms
1 broccoli head
1 onion
1 ginger clove
2 cups water
1 cup organic broth
1-2 teaspoons of miso
Tofu (optional)
2-3 carrots (optional)
2-3 stalks of celery (optional)
Sea veggie flakes to garnish
Sesame seeds to garnish
Spring onions to garnish

DIRECTIONS

- Simmer mushrooms, broccoli, onion, ginger, garlic, water, organic broth or water.
- Add 1 or more heaping teaspoons of miso, tofu (optional), and carrots/celery (optional).
- Garnish with sea veggie flakes, sesame seeds, and green onion.

Medicine – Burdock Tea

ELEMENTAL GROWTH TIP:

Burdock has been an important botanical in Western folk herbalism and traditional Chinese medicine for thousands of years. The root, leaf, and seed are used to make medicine. In tea or tincture, Burdock can increase urine flow, kill germs, reduce fever, and "purify" our blood. Other times we apply burdock directly to the skin for wrinkles, dry skin (ichthyosis), acne, psoriasis, and eczema.

WHAT YOU NEED

½ teaspoon peppermint leaves
½ teaspoon burdock root

DIRECTIONS

- Mix in 1 cup of hot water.
- Allow to steep for a few minutes.
- Enjoy plain or with some raw honey or stevia.

Beauty – Juniper Infused Witch Hazel

ELEMENTAL GROWTH TIP:

Juniper is a natural skin toner and reduces the appearance of skin blemishes. It can also diminish stretch marks and help skin conditions that occur because of hormonal imbalance.

WHAT YOU NEED

1 tablespoon juniper berry infused witch hazel
1 tablespoon aloe vera gel
3 drops lavender essential oil

DIRECTIONS

- Fill a dark jar with dried juniper berries.
- Top with witch hazel and infuse for 1-2 weeks.
- Once completely infused, feel free to use as toner on your face and body once post shower.

MOVEMENT

In this Elemental Growth protocol, we include movement in various forms depending on the season it is and the things you already enjoy doing. Movement will help you heal, reach your health goals, and also release your pain, thoughts, and emotions, in turn enabling you to free your soul and live up to your fullest potential.

It can be hard to motivate yourself to move each day when its cold, dreary, wet, with very little daylight. However, when you take action regardless of what the weather may be outdoors, you may find that everything gets better from your health to your mind and body.[1]

The key is momentum—building it and sustaining it. Yes, going to the gym one to three days a week for an hour is a great resolution, but to get the results you desire and to feel good both inside and out, you must put the work in every single day. I'm not talking about an hour of intense exercise however good that will make you feel, I'm talking about incorporating freeform movement every day to release tension, stress, balance your hormones, and give you a better quality of life.

Now you may think to yourself, I don't have time to work out or I don't have the energy to work out or you may even think, It's been so long since I've worked out or _____ (insert activity here). However, this is no reason to worry. Start with small, actionable, fun activities and work your way up. This applies to the intensity of your physical activity, the time you spend on it, and the number of times you show up consistently for it.

Take a look at what you have already. You have a body that is capable of so much more than you give it credit for. You have music readily available through various me-

---

1 Harvard Health Publishing. "The Wonders of Winter Workouts." Harvard Health Publishing, Harvard Medical School, Dec. 2018, www.health.harvard.edu/staying-healthy/the-wonders-of-winter-workouts.

diums such as a smartphone, radio, your laptop. And you have furniture (chair, bed, couch) and walls. Now contemplate your rituals and habits. There is a better chance that you will stick to a new habit if you tie it to something else you already do every day. This maybe taking a morning shower, brushing your teeth, drinking your morning coffee or a habit you want to break like quitting smoking or yelling out of frustration.

Choose a movement you like—one that will motivate and inspire you to show up for yourself. It may be some form of dance, yoga, pilates, or HIIT workouts that include crunches and cardio. Maybe you like variety and want to designate each day to something different. There is no right or wrong answer here, all you need to do is take action to get started and maintain the momentum to show up for yourself every day. Some of my favorite resources include:

- *Yoga for Real Life* by Maya Fiennes and the *Journey Through The Chakras* video set available on Amazon.com and MayaFiennes.com
- Onnit Academy - Available on Youtube and Onnit.com
- 7-minute Workout App - Available on iTunes and Google Play

Lastly, don't underestimate the power of simply dancing and jumping around to your favorite music playlist on Youtube, iTunes or Amazon music.

CHECK-IN ACTIVITIES

There is a lot less to look at in the winter as the sky is dark and there is a lustrous blanket of white covering the trees and ground. Nature is asking us to go inside, to go within, to reflect and renew our spirit, body, and mind. Winter is the perfect time to turn inwards. We are asked to cocoon ourselves, nurture and nourish ourselves—not exactly to hide out inside our homes, but dive deep into our heart and soul. With a shift in perspective, you may also see that the early nights may actually be a symbol of comfort during the cold and snowy months.

    A great way to embrace this time of year is to create a vision board—casting your vision, your intentions for the year ahead by using pictures, words, quotes that not only inspire you, but they also act as expanders, as markers of where you envision yourself. Making a vision board is a process unique to each individual. Some like to create one all by themselves, while others do it with a friend or two, and some host vision board parties either online or in person. Since *The Secret* revealed the power of vision boards in 2006, you may have an idea of what it is or perhaps even tried it out for yourself already, but I am proposing the idea a little differently because there is value here, even for the skeptics.

    I'm not going to tell you that you can just stick some photos on a board and you will get exactly what you want. What I will tell you is this: When you set an intention behind every single word, picture, quote, affirmation that you have on your vision board, it becomes a powerful tool to help manifest your visions, making them a reality sooner rather than later. There is a science behind visualization, which is why I believe vision boards are an incredible tool. Visualization is essential in maximizing your brain and potential. In fact, we stimulate the same regions in our brain when we visualize an action and when we actually perform that same action.

    The *HuffPost* said it best: *"Tell your brain your plan in a thousand words, and it gets bored mid-way and wants to go to sleep. But draw it a picture, and it will respond with much deeper interest and attention."* When we make vision boards, we not only draw a picture but remind ourselves to practice visualization which then helps to prepare you for the changes you are choosing to make.

    When we get obsessed with something, enough is never enough. We eat, sleep, and breathe whatever it is until we have it. When something seems unrealistic however, this obsession doesn't always click in, the drive to turn passion into action needs fuel. For us, that fuel is learning to believe in ourselves—our ability to make our visions our reality and a sure fire way to generate enough self-belief and self-confidence is to practice visualization with intent and purpose.

    You can generate belief in other ways too, try out one or more of these and let us know what works for you by tagging #ElementalGrowth so we can find you and support you.

- Change your login passwords to an affirmation like "IamFIT&FAB," "Fear2Excitment" or "I<3myLife."

- Draw or paint your dreams and frame them for your wall. Create a digital collage and set it as your wallpaper. Some easy to use tools for this are Canva, DesignBold, Easil, Over, Pinterest to name a few.

- Record a meditation of your goals and listen to them while visualizing yourself already there, successful and grateful.

- Read memoirs of others who resonate with you or tune into a channel like Evan Carmichael on YouTube who creates videos of inspired messages from icons like Joe Rogan, Oprah Winfrey, Alan Watts, Steve Jobs and many more that did it.

Be The Change

    As a way to check in with yourself, schedule weekly and monthly dates with yourself to track your progress. Keep a "win" list to commemorate your visions that have already manifested and use that as another visualization tool to help you propel further towards your goals. It's easy to boost our self-confidence and belief in ourselves when we have a list of all our wins to remind us of how far we've come and how much we've grown.

CHAPTER 2
Spring Clean (Water)

"Spring is nature's way of saying, 'Let's party!'"
— Robin Williams

Spring is governed by the element earth which is symbolic of rebirth. Although we become more lively during this time of year, we may still be stuck indoors more often than we like, as we get a lot of rain in the first few months. This rain helps to thaw out ground that has been frozen all winter, feed the wildlife, and grow foliage for the rest of the year. You may also call it a spring cleaning.

There are many holidays we celebrate in spring as well such as April Fools Day, Earth Day, Arbour Day, Mother's Day, Father's Day, Cinco de Mayo, and Easter to name a few. Spring truly is a symbol of rebirth and should be celebrated. It is a time to make way for the new things that await us, a time to truly play and be one with Mother Nature through a different lens.

Spring bloom may make for a more fun title, but spring doesn't start out that way. The rain first washes away the old, stagnant debris from the year before. Microbes and fungi transforms all that no longer serves us and animals bring life back to the forest, fields, and skies.

As one of Mother Nature's creatures, we too are born again and can follow the same steps. Most homeowners may already have a spring cleaning ritual for their home, but what about cleansing ourselves internally? In this chapter, I will share with you the Elemental Growth protocol for spring cleaning your body, mind, and soul.
Take some time here to ask yourself:

Be The Change

What have I been hanging on to?
What am I willing to release this spring?
How do I intend to fill this cleansed space?
What do I hope will bloom?

_____
_____
_____
_____
_____

SPRING EQUINOX

On the equinox, the sunrise and sunset are twelve hours apart. Daylight and night are almost equal everywhere on earth. This is a time when hibernating bears become active, birds return to sing in the north, and many of nature's creatures have their babies.

The spring equinox has been celebrated as a time of renewal and rebirth for thousands of years. Spring rain and warmth breathes color and life back to the Earth. It's the time to get outside, connect, and observe all the new life beginning around you. You can celebrate by sowing seeds, planting flowers, or building a garden. A bonfire is another great way to celebrate the equinox—tell stories, dance, sing, beat drums, play music, and celebrate the spring with loved ones or even by yourself. Hosting a spring equinox ceremony is an Elemental way you can welcome new life, give thanks for what has passed, and honor transformation at it's finest.

To restore balance in your home environment, do some deep cleaning. Get rid of clutter and anything that you no longer need to make space for the new you.

Donate any material items you haven't used in more than six months. Burn old receipts, paperwork that is no longer needed, and old journals. Join our twenty-eight day coaching event and dedicate at least one hour every day or a few hours each week to go declutter and deep clean each room / section in your home. To balance your mind and body, meditate or practice some yoga, this will cleanse and create inner peace. Use this space to develop a new routine and wish list for the months ahead.

To track your success over this time, take a look at your calendar and ask yourself the following questions: *Where was I at Christmas? Where was I on New Year's Day?* Note when and how you celebrated your holidays. Notice how you felt, your mindset and goals at the time. Focus on the positive and breath out anything else. Now set out to create a meaningful celebration ritual for you and your family.

MOON CYCLES

The moon influences many things on Earth from the ocean tides to our mood and hormonal cycles. The moon can affect our emotions, sleep, and energy. It may also indirectly influence your work life, relationships, and self-care. Let's bring awareness to these days and how the moon influences you.

Many people comment that they are more accident prone, emotional, or erratic during a full moon. Using this time to practice grounding in the form of dance, yoga or breath work can help to balance your emotions during this part of the cycle. During the new moon, you may experience insights from within, thus making it the perfect time for meditation, journaling, or to do something creative.

NEW MOON

The new moon is the first of the lunar phases, and represents a time to ask and manifest. The new moon is when seeds are planted and intentions set. It carries fresh energy that may spark clarity, purpose, and magic within us. Though the sky is dark during this time, when we turn inward, we become our own light.

FULL MOON

Spring is a season that invites fertility, abundance, rebirth, and regrowth. Our behavior may change during the full moon as we become more active and the days become longer. This time is best utilized to revisit our winter resolutions and track our progress. Ask yourself:

What is paying off?

_____
_____
_____
_____
_____

What isn't working for you right now?

_____
_____
_____
_____
_____

- **Full Pink Moon:** April's pink moon is named after Phlox, a stunning star-shaped wildflower. These plants are one of the first perennials to bloom in spring. Phlox flowers symbolize friendship, harmony, and sweet dreams. This full moon is the perfect time to take an inventory of your friends, home, mind and body, and cleanse what no longer serves you and encourage new growth.

- **Full Flower Moon:** Many more wildflowers begin blooming in May and they will continue to spring up in abundance. This full moon is the time to focus on beauty and clear out some of the remnants from the previous months.

- **Full Strawberry Moon:** June is named after one of our favorite berry picking seasons: strawberry. Strawberries are a sign that the heat of summer is arriving and represents Venus, the Goddess of love. Use this full moon to align with what feels right for you. Check-in with the people, places, and things that open your heart and release all that's left behind.

CIRCADIAN RHYTHM

Our circadian rhythm doesn't only influence when we sleep but many other biological functions including energy, mood, physical activity, hormone levels, body temperature, immune function, and digestive activity. Problems often begin when our master clock is out of sync. A great habit to form during Spring is to begin a simple form of intermittent fasting. This means limiting the hours of the day when you eat. There are many methods of intermittent fasting but to keep it simple, aim to eat all your meals and snacks within an eight to ten hour window earlier in the day. For best results, take it a step further and aim to eat breakfast within an hour of waking up and stop eating at least two hours before you go to sleep.

According to Harvard University, intermittent fasting can help weight loss too and after just five weeks, can dramatically lower insulin levels, improve insulin sensitivity, lower blood pressure, and regulate your appetite.[2]

- **April:** Daylight between 7:00am and 7:45pm
- **May:** Daylight between 6:30am and 8pm
- **June**: Daylight between 6:30am and 8:15pm

FOOD GUIDE & RECIPES

By now, your healthy food plan should focus on nutrient-dense foods such as whole fruits, vegetables, herbs and wildfoods. You may have discovered a newfound love for seasonal eating and understand that it's not about what we are eliminating but instead, how much our diet is expanding with new delicious and nutritious foods.

The Doctrine of Signatures is an approach to healthy eating that connects foods found in nature to individual body parts.[3] Healthy eating is quite simple when we insist on it being that way. During spring, I often focus my effort on this approach because it allows me to perceive the benefits of what I consume in a new way. It allows us to ask questions like: *Will eating this allow me to grow or hinder my efforts toward self-improvement?*

Flip over for some of our favorite spring foods, recipes, remedies, and tinctures for Elemental Growth, enjoy!

---

2 Tello, Monique. "Intermittent Fasting: Surprising Update." Harvard Health Blog, Harvard Health Publishing, 26 June 2018, www.health.harvard.edu/blog/intermittent-fasting-surprising-update-2018062914156.

3 "Doctrine of Signatures." Elemental Growth, 26 Mar. 2019, elementalgrowth.org/doctrine-of-signatures/.

Breakfast - Banana Crepes

INGREDIENTS

2 cups gluten-free flour
2 cups plant-based milk (or water)
2 mashed bananas
Salt to taste
Cinnamon to taste

DIRECTIONS

- Place all the ingredients in a bowl. Whisk them all together using a whisk or electric mixer until you have a smooth batter.
- Lightly grease a medium frying pan with some coconut or avocado oil and heat the pan until hot.
- Pour about 4 tablespoons of batter into the pan and swirl it around to ensure even coverage.
- Fry on each side until golden.
- Enjoy plain or with some homemade condiments and fruit toppings (see next page for condiment recipe).

Condiments

PEANUT BUTTER

- Blend roasted, unsalted peanuts until desired texture is achieved.
- Feel free to add other nuts seeds, cocoa, or natural sweeteners as you desire, but from my experience, simple is best.

CHIA SEED JAM

- Blend 2 cups of chopped fruit, 1 tablespoon lemon juice, 1 tablespoon maple syrup, and 2 tablespoons chia seeds.
- Chill overnight. This recipe lasts one week in the fridge.

ALTERNATIVES FOR TOPPINGS

Experiment with:

- A mashed avocado topped with hemp seeds
- Mashed banana with cinnamon
- Some of our other condiment recipes found online at www.elementalgrowth.org

ASHLEY MICHAUD

AM Snack - Frozen Strawberry Lemonade

INGREDIENTS

1 lemon (freshly squeezed juice)
2 teaspoons maple syrup
1 cup frozen strawberries
1 banana

DIRECTIONS

- Blend all ingredients and enjoy chilled!

Lunch – Rainbow Kale Salad

INGREDIENTS

1 bunch fresh kale
1 bulb of purple garlic
1 red onion
2 carrots
1 yellow pepper
1 serving of raisins
1 cup flax seeds
1 cup sunflower seeds
1 cup cooked rice or quinoa
Olive oil
Himalyan sea salt to taste.

DIRECTIONS

- Chop and massage kale with olive oil and Himalayan sea salt.
- Add red onion, carrot, yellow pepper, broccoli, raisins, purple garlic, cooked rice/quinoa, pumpkin seeds, flax seeds, and sunflower seeds.
- Mix together with salad dressing and enjoy chilled.

ASHLEY MICHAUD

Creamy Avo Salad Dressing

INGREDIENTS

1 ripe avocado
1 tablespoon apple cider vinegar
1 teaspoon maple syrup
Himalayan sea salt (to taste)

DIRECTIONS

- Mix 1 mashed avocado, Himalayan sea salt, apple cider vinegar, and maple syrup.
- Garnish with purple sauerkraut.

ELEMENTAL GROWTH TIP:

- I love making homemade sauerkraut and find that it tastes so good when mixed with the avocado in this salad. Sauerkraut is easy to make and loaded in probiotics (by definition meaning "life force") which help heal and maintain a healthy gut biome.
- Recipe found at www.elementalgrowth.org/Recipe-Share

PM Snack - Beet Chips

INGREDIENTS

3-5 beetroots
Coconut / avocado oil
Himalayan sea salt (to taste)
Spices of your choice (for seasoning)

DIRECTIONS

- Slice beetroot thinly using a processor or mandoline then marinate in oil, salt, and spices of choice.
- Bake at 300 degrees for 45-60 minutes. These will store well for two weeks.

ELEMENTAL GROWTH TIP:

- Coconut oil and avocado oil can both be used for cooking or baking recipe that require extreme heat or high temperatures.
- They are both rich in vitamin A, C, E, and D, and have multiple uses ranging from cooking to hair and skin-care nourishment.

Supper – Pesto Pasta

INGREDIENTS

1/3 cup cashews
1/3 cup coconut oil
1 bulb of garlic
1/3 cup nutritional yeast
Microgreens of your choice
Whole rice pasta or spaghetti squash or spiralized zucchini

DIRECTIONS

- Add 1/3 cup cashews, 1/3 cup coconut oil, head of garlic, and 1/3 cup nutritional yeast together and blend together in your food processor and top it off with micro-greens of choice.
- Simmer the sauce and pour over spaghetti squash, spiralized zucchini or whole rice pasta. Top with vegan cashew parmesan cheese (recipe below).

Vegan Cashew Parmesan Cheese

INGREDIENTS

¾ cup cashews
3 tablespoons nutritional yeast
Himlayan sea salt (to taste)
1 bulb of garlic

DIRECTIONS

- Blend 3 tablespoons nutritional yeast, ¾ cup cashews, garlic, and Himalayan sea salt together in your food processor.
- Crumble on your pasta dish. Refrigerate any leftover cheese.

Medicine – Dandelion Coffee

ELEMENTAL GROWTH TIP:

Dandelion is far more than a weed and a flower. It is a highly nutritious source of food and medicine. We use dandelions during spring because they are in full bloom and an amazing cleanser. Dandelion is high in antioxidants, fight inflammation, detoxes the body, and purifies the blood and liver.

WHAT YOU NEED

1½ tablespoons dried dandelion root (less if you are using powder)
Coconut cream (optional)
Natural sweetener (optional)
Cinnamon, ginger, vanilla (optional)

DIRECTIONS

- Boil all ingredients together.
- Add plant based milk if desired.
- Enjoy hot!

Beauty – Pretty Plantain Oil

ELEMENTAL GROWTH TIP:

Plantain leaves can heal wounds, stop itching, kill bad germs and bacteria, and generate new and healthy skin cells. This recipe is easy but requires love and intention.

WHAT YOU NEED

Plantain leaves
Olive oil
Mason jar
Window
Cheesecloth
Sea salt (optional)

DIRECTIONS

- Fill a mason jar with plantain leaves and cover with olive oil.
- Set this in your window for 2 weeks.
- Drain your oil through cheesecloth and use as a face serum or mix your infused oil with sea salt and use as a body scrub.

ASHLEY MICHAUD

MOVEMENT

When I began learning Kundalini yoga, there was a moment when I understood how energy gets locked in our body and how movement was the key to releasing pain both physically and emotionally. I have experienced this time and time again through my practice and in everyday life. It's like an awakening that brightens the soul, sheds family karma, and releases any pain we have endured in this lifetime.

Now that the days are getting longer, the air a bit warmer, and the rains wash away the remnants of last year, we too should consider shaking up and releasing stagnant energy through some movement. Increase the amount of exercise you do in a day by adding in a nightly yoga routine, a nature walk, or run around the block.

You have gained momentum from your winter resolutions which is often the hardest part. Now that you've started incorporating physical activity into your daily routine, I encourage you to celebrate how far you have come. Strike a yoga pose in your backyard, turn the music loud and dance with whoever is around. Release can feel intense at times, which is why it is important to focus on the positive in your day. Bring out your inner child to play and celebrate you for the miracle that you are!

I believe that movement can help anyone feel this way even if it's not from a yoga practice. Everything varies from one person to the next. We are all very unique and for this reason, exploring various forms of movement will help us identify with one that brings us joy while helping us stay consistent. Now that things are heating up, we have more options opening up to us. What are some outdoor activities that you can integrate into your day?

It doesn't matter what we choose to do, as long as we can bring awareness to your breath. Breath is the life force of energy. The average person cannot last more than three minutes without oxygen, to put that into perspective, consider this: We can go at least twenty-one days (three weeks) without food or water. Using different breathing techniques throughout our day serves many benefits and also cleanses our body. Some of our favorite breathing techniques include:

- **Lion's Breath**: Blow off some steam, wake up your face, and brighten your day with this silly and detoxifying breathing exercise. Breath in deeply and breathe out deeply through your mouth, tongue stretched out.
- **Breath of Fire**: Sniffing in and out through our nose can detoxify the body of anger, stress, and overwhelming feelings. To create balance in the body, place your thumb on one nostril and pinkie on the other, switching back and forth with a rhythm that feels right for you.

And don't forget to bring awareness to your breath in other ways that feel right for you. Any movement you do can be aligned to your breath, and from my personal experience, the more aligned you are with your breath, the more health and happiness will come your way. So breathe on, my friend!

CHECK-IN ACTIVITIES

Spring represents new beginnings. Perennials are coming back to life, trees are budding, and greens are sprouting out of the ground. Everywhere we look, the colors and energies are changing from death to rebirth. Spring is a time when we can break free from the stagnancy of winter and move forward into the next chapter of your life.

If you are struggling with a health issue that you are ready to release, finding it hard to hold yourself accountable for your diet and exercise routine or seeking direction and clarity—now is the time to breakaway from limiting beliefs and habits, and take intentional action towards your dreams. Spring is the time to organize your ideas, intentions, drawers, cupboards, and closets. It's the time to reclaim your mind, life, environment, and free your spirit.

Are you aware of when you're feeding your soul too much junk to feel good? Do you lose time by constantly patrolling your social feeds, compulsively digging into the latest gossip, video games, or binge-watching Netflix? These types of activities can seriously drain your spiritual energy. During the spring months, we recommend that you surround yourself with people who make you laugh and genuinely make you happy. Laughter is the most powerful medicine and soul food. When you are in the company of those who make your light shine brighter, don't question it, just enjoy them. Truly relish their presence and let their infectious laughter and dynamic energy rub off on you.

Focus on the things you enjoy about the people closest to you, it's important to remember that the things we see in others are also reflections of ourselves. Practicing random acts of kindness allows you to receive an act of kindness. Did you know that when we give, our body releases serotonin? This means that when we feed others kindness and nurture them, we nourish our soul as well in the process.

When we consider external forces, many of us are being overrun by toxins in the air, food, water, cleaning supplies, and personal care products. Over time, the toxic effects of these factors can add up, increasing our toxic overload. You can begin crowding out your home by adding in more natural products and experimenting with some DIY recipes at www.elementalgrowth.org. With time, this practice will become effortless.

Throughout the spring, slowly go each room within your home and make it your own. Take everything that doesn't serve the new you and box it up. Cleanse your space. Gretchen Rubin (author of *The Happiness Project*) recommends that each room has an empty shelf, and everything that makes you feel anything but light should go to another home. As you continue to create space in your home, remember that you are not your past, you are the person who has learned, grown, and gotten your priorities in order. This is an abundant world and you already have everything you need within you. Just trust the process and make the purge.

As you cleanse your inner and outer worlds, you may be wondering what to do with all your stuff. I often find that a smudging / burning ritual is a beneficial way to cleanse old stagnant energy, while donating items away is an efficient and rewarding way to detox your physical world.

Another fun way to spring clean your home is by organizing a party with friends to help you go through your home. In my experience, this is the most fun way of doing a spring cleaning and your friends usually take everything you want to get rid of with them as they leave. Good luck spring cleaners, may good vibes and positivity guide you through this transformational process.

CHAPTER 3

Summer Love (Fire)

"It's hard to see with the sun in your eyes but one day you're going to say, 'I saw the light.'"
– Kid Rock, Roll On

Around the world, we celebrate summer in the form of festivals, for you, this may be at your local beach or around the picnic table. Some rituals are for fertility, while others symbolize the season of growth, full bloom, and daylight. Summertime also opens up many new forms of activities such as boating, camping, skinny dipping or a moonlight stroll through town.

What kind of activities do you find yourself involved in this time of year?

What areas of your life can use some extra love?

_____
_____
_____
_____
_____

Summer is governed by the element of fire which symbolizes our spirit, willpower, and the sun. Nature is beautiful and fruitful at this time of year. Fruits burst from flowers, the sun peaks, and our activities go on later into the night. Summertime allows animals and plants to reproduce and for all Mother Nature's creatures to store enough energy and nutrition for the cold months to come.

Summer's comfortable conditions open new opportunities to forage, fish, and enjoy other outdoor activities. Having access to the warming sun, flowing water, fresh air, and fertile soil provides us the ingredients we need for health, happiness, and Elemental Growth.

The sun is vital for balancing our mood, circadian rhythm, and producing Vitamin D, which acts more like a hormone than a vitamin because it affects every cell in our body. Some say that "the summer rain washes away the pain," and I have to agree and add that summer is nature's version of radical self-love.

Self-love is not a selfish act, as you can see from Mother Nature, self-love is rooted in giving back. Take the time this summer to support your local farmers, spend some time attending local community events, and create a mindset shift that allows you to give and receive freely. It's time to create a ripple effect of radical self-love for every single soul you interact with, every single life you touch and impact.

What are some ways you can practice self-love this summer? List at least ten ways you will show yourself some self-love.

_____

_____

_____

_____

_____

_____

_____

ASHLEY MICHAUD

SOLSTICE

Summer is the hottest of the four seasons and has the longest days and shortest nights. This is the best time to celebrate yourself and the progress you have made through the year. Many people do this already in the form of a vacation, but some others may need a little push. Summer is an opportunity for families to celebrate, bond, and add new rituals to their lives. Some cool ideas are: hosting a scavenger hunt, having a picnic, practicing yoga outdoors, scratching something off your bucket list, star gazing, taking a moonlight stroll, going for a swim, enjoying community hot-spots or a good old hosedown in your yard, getting dirty, and getting out with your family / community.

    Summer is governed by the element of fire which is actually my favorite even though I am an air sign. I love the fire because it is the element we must create within ourselves. An easy way to experience this is to rub your hands together really fast to create heat and stimulate the energy within you. Another way is to dance, move or do work that lights you up from the inside out—Fire represents our spirit!

    Use this time to discover and zone in on what lights you up and harness what fuels your spirit. Proper nutrition, exercise, and loving connections are all incredible fuel sources but these alone cannot solve all your problems. Its by aligning with your natural energy—the unique energy that you were born with so that you can bring harmony to your mind, body, and spirit.

    Summer solstice represents ascension, prosperity, and good vibes. Our summer solstice ritual has been inspired by this symbology as we often gather around a big bonfire which we light in the early morning and burn until nightfall. We invite everyone over to share food, music, and laughter. We also invite our guests to write down their golden intentions and allow them to transform from thought to paper, paper to fire, fire to ash, and so on . . . I now invite you too, to join us in our summer solstice ritual by using the #ElementalGrowth when you share your pictures and videos so we can find you and support your Elemental Growth journey.

MOON CYCLES

During a full moon, your state of mind is important because everything becomes magnified—good and bad. As you progress in your Elemental Growth journey, it's wise to ground yourself with meditation so that you can see this as a time of opportunity. It's up to you to cultivate the good vibes and positivity you seek.

The moon symbolises water and influence over the tides. The moon's influence shows up within us too: in our emotions, intuition, and sacral chakra center. When we tap into this and the other elements at work during summer time, we become cosmically conscious thus finding it easier to hear nature's secret messages.

NEW MOON

In the still and dark night what do you see? Hear? Feel? Take some time to reflect on how far you have come and the lessons you have picked up along the way. Your journey is progressing but far from over. It's now time to make new plans and set those plans into motion.

FULL MOON

Take the opportunity this summer to bath in the round and completely illuminated moonlight. Observe and apply your findings to your own life. The full moon represents completion, the height of power, self-realization, and clarity. It is a time to dance and celebrate your Elemental Growth journey.

- **Full Buck Moon:** Also called Thundermoon or Mead moon. Like all the moons, there can be many names and while I love the many thunderstorms this time of year, the Buck totem represents regeneration which is happening all around us.
- **Full Sturgeon Moon:** Named after the fishing season, this moon also reminds us that we are safe and protected. The sturgeon is also one of the longest living freshwater fish and symbolises wisdom.
- **Full Harvest Moon:** This is the closest full moon to the fall equinox and symbolizes a time of peace. Spend this time with your family, take a nature walk together, prepare a nice meal from the local harvest and you will feel it too.

CIRCADIAN RHYTHM

According to Matthew Walker, sleep is the best optimization tool to boost performance and its legal as well as free. Our quality of sleep can get affected for many reasons ranging from ageism to non stop screen time, however, a major culprit that impacts sleep quality is stress. For many of my clients, stress easily turns into late nights, then late nights turn into less productivity followed by more stress. Getting in tune with our circadian rhythm can break this cycle and like Matthew Walker talks about, actually optimize our life.

The late nights and busy days that parallel this wonderful season can add both physical and mental stress to our body, mind, and spirit. Cortisol, also known as the "stress hormone" comes in really handy when we are in danger and is at its peak when we first wake up. Cortisol will naturally taper off throughout the day, but for many with an out of whack circadian rhythm, their cortisol levels can fluctuate rapidly throughout the day causing them to have insomnia or wake up several times through the night.

The goal in summer time is to help your body release this energy by getting outside for the morning sunrise and by relaxing in bed, free of electronics, before 10pm. The sunrise will revive your pineal gland which is responsible for melatonin functions, also known as the third-eye, while going to bed before 10pm will ensure that melatonin is released before the inevitable 10pm second wind.

- **July:** Daylight between 5:50am and 8:55pm
- **August:** Daylight between 6:20am and 8:20pm
- **September:** Daylight between 6:55am and 7:30pm

FOOD GUIDES & RECIPES

Summer is a time of fruits. In essence, it's time that we harvest the fruits of our labor. If we know what to look for and where to look, summer foraging opportunities are everywhere and if foraging is not for you, check out a local farmers' market and stock up on the goods in bulk while they are fresh and less expensive.

While drying food in a dehydrator can make them last longer and a wonderful summer activity, fermentation is the best way of preserving food because it increases the nutrient quantity by introducing living probiotic cultures into our gut. We have more gut bacteria than we do cells in our body and these bacteria make up 98% of our serotonin (happy chemicals). On our weekly recipe share, you will often see me posting recipes such as these so that you can experience health through a balanced microbiome.

On the next page are some of our favorite summer foods, recipes, remedies, and tinctures for Elemental Growth, enjoy!

Breakfast – Sweet Avocado Boats

With Berries and Dark Chocolate Drizzle

INGREDIENTS

Berries of your choice
Cacao powder or paste
¼ cup coconut oil
½ cup plant based milk
Agave or honey to sweeten
Vanilla essence
Sea salt to taste

DIRECTIONS

- Cut an avocado in half lengthwise and remove the core.

FOR CHOCOLATE DRIZZLE:

- Melt ¼ cup coconut oil in a small pot over the stove top on a low heat.
- Next, add cacao powder, ½ cup plant based milk, agave or honey, vanilla essence, and sea salt.
- Whisk until there are no lumps of cacao powder and the agave or honey has mixed well with the rest of the mixture.
- Refrigerate in a mason jar to enjoy for future meals.
- Fill the avocado with some berries of your choice, drizzle some dark chocolate goodness, and enjoy this brain boosting breakfast.

Breakfast – Savory Avocado Boats

Avocado Boats with Chickpea Mash

INGREDIENTS

1 can chickpeas
1 stalk of celery
2 spring onions
1 red pepper
½ teaspoon garlic powder
Mustard (to your liking)
Red sauerkraut

DIRECTIONS

- Cut an avocado in half lengthwise and remove the core.
- Fill the avocado with some filling(s) of your choice and enjoy this brain boosting breakfast.
- Mash chickpeas and mix in some celery, green onion, red pepper, garlic powder and mustard.
- Fill boat with mixture and top with red sauerkraut (red cabbage in a salt water brine).

ASHLEY MICHAUD

AM Snack – Hulk Bowls

INGREDIENTS

2 frozen bananas
1 teaspoon spirulina powder
1 cup mashed berries
¼ cup chia seeds
Hemp seeds
Honey to taste

DIRECTIONS

- Blend up two frozen bananas with one teaspoon of spirulina.
- Take it a step further and top it with a blackberry chia jam (see below for instructions).

Blackberry Chia Jam

INGREDIENTS

1 cup blackberries (mashed)
¼ cup chia seeds
1 tablespoon honey

DIRECTIONS

- In a bowl, mix 1 cup of mashed blackberries, ¼ cup chia seeds, and honey to create a delicious filling and spread that is full of antioxidant goodness along with healthy fats and omegas.
- Add a sprinkle with hemp seeds and enjoy!

Lunch – Summer Love Salad

INGREDIENTS

1 cup cooked quinoa
1 cup wild rice
1 bunch of kale
1 bunch persulane
1 cup blueberries
1 cup Concord grapes
½ cup walnuts
½ cup sunflower seeds
Honey to taste
Balsamic vinegar to taste

DIRECTIONS

- Combine quinoa, wild rice, kale, persulane, blueberries, Concord grapes, sunflower seeds, and walnuts.
- Drizzle with honey and balsamic vinegar. Enjoy chilled.

PM Snack – Dark Chocolate Popcorn

INGREDIENTS

½ cup dried corn kernels
2 tablespoons coconut oil
Coconut flakes (as desired)
Dark chocolate drizzle

DIRECTIONS

- Heat a pot with a drop or more or oil, add in some dried corn kernels and cover.
- Shake every couple minutes until all the corn is popped.
- Mix in coconut flakes and some dark chocolate drizzle (see recipe for dark chocolate drizzle under: Avocado Boats with Berries and Dark Chocolate Drizzle).

Supper – Garden Grill Platter & Burgers

Gather everything from the garden, fridge, and your imagination. Heat up the bbq or light a fire it's grilling time! The ingredients listed below are what I typically use to create a nourishing, filling, and tasty garden grill platter. Feel free to use as much or as little as you desire. This is one meal that does not require exact measurements. Any extra leftovers can be enjoyed for another meal or two.

INGREDIENTS

Zucchini (as much as you desire)
Mushrooms (you can pick any variety you desire, portabella mushrooms are ideal)
Corn
Peppers (red, green, yellow)
Pineapple

DIRECTIONS

Zucchini: Slice it, spice it, and coat with some chickpea flour for an extra crispy bite.

Mushrooms: Marinate with balsamic vinegar or liquid aminos and your favorites herbs overnight.

Corn: Soak whole corn (husk on) in a sink of water for twenty minutes or longer and then throw stick on the grill. Once cooked, you can remove the husk and add all the flavorings you like. For a savory platter, add some cayenne, lemon, salt, and pepper to give your corn on the cob some zesty flavor.

Peppers: For small peppers, chop off the top and for bigger ones, slice them lengthwise. Stuff them with vegan feta (sprouted almonds, apple cider vinegar, garlic and salt) or coat them in coconut oil and spices.

Pineapple: Slice pineapple and grill. Take it to the next level and add some chipotle seasoning.

Burgers: There are so many ways to make a delicious vegan burger, but here's our latest craze: broccoli and lentil burgers. See next page for additional recipe.

Broccoli and Lentil Burgers

Don't let these ingredients fool you. This recipe will make you fall in love with vegan burgers as it is juicy, tasty, and full of nutrients.

INGREDIENTS

1 cup of sprouted red lentils
1 cup of broccoli
¼ cup mushrooms
¼ cup onion
¼ cup puffed brown rice
3 tablespoons chia seeds
1 teaspoon coriander powder or fresh coriander leaves
1 teaspoon cumin powder or cumin seeds
Sea salt to taste

DIRECTIONS

- In a food processor, combine 1 cup of sprouted red lentils, 1 cup of broccoli, ¼ cup mushrooms, ¼ cup onion, ¼ cup puffed brown rice, 3 tablespoons chia seeds, coriander, cumin, and salt.
- Create patties and cook them on a cast iron pan with a steel spatula to make sure they stay together.
- Enjoy with your choice of wholegrain or gluten-free bread. Another amazing substitute for gluten-free bread is portobello mushrooms as your burger buns.

Medicine – Poison Ivy Prevention & Remedy

ELEMENTAL GROWTH TIP:

Once you harvest your jewelweed, let it sweat for a few days or put it into the dehydrator. Add the flowers to a colored glass jar and cover in your favorite carrier oil (almond, olive, sunflower or avacado are great choices).

WHAT YOU NEED

Jewelweed
Your choice of carrier oil
Beeswax (optional if you want to make a cream)

DIRECTIONS

- Set this in the window for a couple of weeks to catch the sun and moon light. You can skip this step and apply fresh flowers or take it to the next level and make a cream by straining the flowers and combining the oil with melted beeswax.

Beauty – Hikers Perfume

ELEMENTAL GROWTH TIP:

This 2oz bottle of perfume will ward off flies, mosquitos, sand fleas, and more. If you get bit as it wears off, apply some apple cider vinegar which will reduce the itch and help your bite heal faster. Witch hazel or tea tree oil will also provide immediate relief.

WHAT YOU NEED

Witch hazel
Carrier oil of choice
10-20 drops lavender essential oil
10-20 drops of eucalyptus essential oil
Water as desired

DIRECTIONS

- Mix witch hazel, carrier oil of choice, 10-20 drops of lavender essential oil and 10-20 drops of eucalyptus essential oil and top the rest with water.

MOVEMENT

A healthy weight is about much more than a number on the scale. During this season as we become more active in our everyday life, let's focus on the other factors that define and determine a healthy weight, such as relationships, activity levels, sleep, medications, and your genetics. Active movement allows us to release pain, thoughts, emotions that may otherwise sit there causing an increase in discomfort and can develop into something more.

Additionally, the website www.23andme.com can provide you with DNA genetic testing right from your home. These results can help you figure out what kind of movement you're made for and tons more about ancestry, health risk, and traits. Use these results to better understand yourself and get answers to many of the questions you have asked yourself over the years.

When it comes to being healthy, which of these factors do you think most affects your ability to maintain a healthy weight outside of food and exercise? What one action can you take this week to nurture this aspect of your life?

Top ways to maintain a healthy weight during the summer:

- **Yard work:** What a great therapy that also reaps the reward. Therapeutic, healing, and invigorating, this may mean raking, working the land or caring for a patio garden.

- **Nature yoga:** Balance on rocks, ask a tree for help to support your inversions and get dirty on the beach.

- **Fire dancing:** A great way to get grounded and enhance your spiritual energy is to host a bonfire and dance like our ancestors.

- **Foraging / Hiking:** These are two of my favorite

summer activities and the very reason I say, "Spread good vibes and wildflowers." During your next nature walk, do the same by inviting a friend or helping the wildflowers spread their seeds.

- **Getting wet:** While some swear by cryotherapy as their secret tool all times of the year, it's more easier to emerge yourself in cold water is during the summertime. Rain or shine, embrace the element of water fully by dancing in the rain, swimming in the bay, and jumping in puddles.

Remember, the goal is not to do everything, but to take what resonates with you and make it your own. Summer is all about loving who you are and what you do!

CHECK-IN ACTIVITIES

I am sure you have heard the phrase, *"You must first love yourself before you are able to give love to others."* While we all have intentions to love freely, such is not always the case. Holding onto past memories and traumas or the strong emotions that are alive within us can make it hard at times to identify if we are giving the ones we love the kind of love they need or reflecting the type of love we are seeking.

Summer is a great time to check-in with yourself about how you treat yourself and others. To ensure that this is a growing experience, I have included our ABC to Self-Love exercise, where you can learn about *The 5 Love Languages* by Gary Chapman and learn how to break through those strong emotions using Ho'oponopono: a forgiveness ritual.

ABC'S TO SELF-LOVE

Affirmations: In spiritual practice, we learn the power

behind the words "I am" which is how I begin most of my personal affirmations. "I am" is a key phrase when practicing affirmations because it represents our identity. When used properly with fervency and intention, it can help us to redefine ourselves and our full potential. Some examples I have used include: "I am completely whole," "I am inspired and in flow," and "I am contagiously positive."

Boundaries: Exploring boundaries that serve you can be grounding for our entire chakra system. Our root chakra is both our foundation and our boundary system. It keeps us from taking on other people's baggage, being too flighty, reduces frustration due to daily stress, and leads the way to self-love so we may connect with our heart and our intuition.

Commandments: Making personal commandments is a practice that was inspired by the best selling author Gretchen Rubin. On her journey to happiness she decided to break her year down into twelve categories, labeling each one a different personal commandment that she would focus on for that month. Order is important so that you don't overextend yourself. For the first month, you will have only your first commandment to work on and by the end of the year, you will have successfully enriched your life with twelve commandments that work to benefit you.

LOVING OTHERS

Understand the language of love: According to Gary Chapman, author of *The 5 Love Languages*, there are five ways in which we give and receive love. Words of affirmation, acts of service, receiving gifts, quality time and physical touch. Take the quiz by yourself or with your loved ones and learn your love language here: https://www.5lovelanguages.com/

Forgive everybody for everything: A powerful affirmation we practice in times of trouble is this: "I forgive everybody for everything." This simple yet powerful statement releases grief and allows loving energy to flow again. In Hawaii, many practice Ho'oponopono (which means "to make it right") to solve problems and conflicts. To practice this yourself, you need only know four magical sentences: I am sorry, please forgive me, I love you, and thank you.

Not So Random Acts of Kindness: The act of giving is much more rewarding than receiving, in fact, studies teach us that no matter how rich or poor one may feel, displaying acts of kindness and generosity bring us more happiness. In the words of Mahatma Gandhi, *"The best way to find yourself is to lose yourself in the service of others."* Doing this in daily life can be as simple as opening a door for someone else, smiling as you pass someone on the street, leaving a tip or finding something funny to lighten someone's day.

A fun way to practice radical self-love and kindness towards yourself and others can be by means of a self-love challenge. Start one yourself by posting a picture of what radical self-love means to you on social media and encourage your friends to join you for thirty days. Before you know it, a self-love mindset will be a conscious part of your day to day activities and can rewire your brain and heart to operate from a place of unconditional positive regard. Don't forget to use #ElementalGrowth so we can support you on your jouney!

CHAPTER 4
Fall Elimination (Air)

ASHLEY MICHAUD

"Winter is an etching, spring a watercolor, summer an oil painting and autumn a mosaic of them all."
– *Stanley Horowitz*

Fall is governed by the element of air and signifies love and balance. It's a time when a cooler breeze arrives to fill our hearts with love and bellies with the summer's harvest. Thanksgiving, Halloween, and Black Friday are the most celebrated fall events. Fall harvest festivals truly fill our cup with good music, celebrations, and food.

Autumn, or as we call it in North America, Fall, named after the many fallen leaves, is when trees show us their true shapes and colors and when plants use their own customized method to spread seeds for the next generation. This is the time to fill our homes and bodies with harvested fruits, nuts, and seeds because most foods can be found in abundance everywhere this time of year.

The fall season is an amazing time of year which brings a unique set of gifts to all Mother Nature's creatures. Animals gather food in preparation for the coming winter, those with fur often grow thicker coats while other species build up their fat reserves for migration or hibernation to survive the falling temperatures.

As the weather begins to get colder, the insects flee, plants stop making food, and animals prepare for the cold months ahead. Yet there is one tree that remains constant—the Evergreen. We can take many lessons from this tree which represents longevity, virtue, and solitude.

As our year comes to a close and shifts back into resolution mode, let's take a minute to check in with ourselves and celebrate each of our shifts and accomplishments.

Is there something you feel ready to let go of?
What are some ways you can fill your cup this fall?

_____
_____
_____
_____
_____

FALL EQUINOX

As summer turns to fall, we heat our homes and layer up with hoodies, blankets, and slippers. We also tend to focus on our health by boosting our immunity through nutrition and building healthy habits. As leaves fall from trees and seeds drop from other plants, we too must consider the beauty of letting go.

This season teaches us that death is merely preparation for rebirth and invites us to apply this concept of death to our egocentric patterns that no longer benefit us. The idea of letting go can be scary, so use this time to observe how beautiful nature's natural cycles can be. She eases into things and is open to help from the wind, wildlife, and fungi—all of which are connected symbiotically.

Fall is the time to practice heightened self-awareness and be observant and aware of one's surroundings. It represents preservation, gathering reserves, creating a cozy environment, and developing new rituals that you can carry forth into winter. These actions give us the chance to reconnect with ourselves as we embrace our ever-changing lives.

ASHLEY MICHAUD

Day and night are the same length during the fall equinox all around the world and governed by sun sign Libra. As a result, ancient cultures have always associated this day with the concept of balance. Use this time to tap into the balance within you by asking yourself these questions:

When do I feel safe?
I feel safe when I _____.

When do I feel most balanced?
I feel most balanced when I _____.

When do I feel warm and fuzzy?
I get a warm feeling inside when I _____.

When do I feel most grounded?
I feel grounded when I _____.

In the space below, write down any questions that come up as you reflect on what balance means to you.

_____
_____
_____
_____
_____
_____

MOON CYCLES

The moon energies are in full force this time of year and by now, I'm sure you have found your own flow when it comes to moon rituals. The full moon often signifies a time of completion, heightened emotions, and illumination, while the new moon highlights new beginnings, imagination, and rebirth.
Now let's take it a step further and notice the moon phases within each moon cycle which are just as much a guide as anything else in nature. The 1st quarter moon arrives one week after the new moon and is symbolic of growth, expansion, and progress. This moon is growing and telling us to stay motivated and take small action steps daily. The 3rd quarter moon comes one week after the full moon and symbolic of letting go and surrendering to the higher good. This is a good time to reflect, contemplate, and release the relationships, negative thoughts, and poor habits that may be keeping you stuck and stagnant so you can pursue your goals with a clear mind.

NEW MOON

Darkness is associated with creative and divine feminine energy. As our blindness heightens the psychic abilities within us, we can tap into this creativity and pull off things we may have never known we were capable of all along. The new moon is a time to tune into our own answers and the infinite potential we can cultivate. Set aside time for intention-setting and create your own new moon ritual.

FULL MOON

The full moon is a good time to use grounding practices to quiet our subconscious mind. Like the illuminating full moon, we too can be the guiding light through the darkness. Go deep this season and tap into your parental nature. Re-parent and nurture yourself. Imagine yourself as a child you must care for, how would you ensure this child is protected, fed, and nurtured?

- **Full Hunter Moon:** Traditionally, hunters would use the light of the full moon to track down their prey and stock up for the coming winter. Tonight's moon may appear bigger and brighter than usual, giving plenty of bright light and warm energy to dance, stroll or bathe in early evening moonlight.

- **Full Beaver Moon:** This is the last full moon before the rivers freeze and is named after the beaver because they get especially busy on this night. Beavers teach us to have a plan and take action on it. Beavers are also a great example of teamwork, which makes it easier to turn our dreams into reality.

- **Full Cold Moon:** This moon is usually associated with the winter solstice and referred to as the "longest night moon." Your intuition will be stronger than normal right now which can guide you in making quick decisions. Follow your instincts and make the most of any opportunities that come your way.

CIRCADIAN RHYTHM

As the summer heat begins to dissipate, you may feel the winter blues setting in. This isn't really for everybody and should not be for anybody because there are natural forces within us that store vitamin D, regulate our mood, and enhance our overall outlook on life.

Mood disorders are among the most common and serious diseases. One of the most common effects is disruptions in sleeping patterns. This can be due to shift work, travel or practicing an unhealthy routine. The food we crave, our immune system, and our hormonal functions are all affected by our mood and sleeping patterns.

Everything is symbiotic which means that if one part is weak, everything becomes a bit weaker and when everything is functioning optimally and each part is strong, you too are strong.

Fall is a great time to strengthen these functions and nature provides us with the answers we seek. Mushrooms are in abundance at this time and they are one of our best food sources for vitamin D. Just about every fruit and root is available, most of which can curb sugar cravings. Fresh berries and the high vitamin C content in cauliflower can help boost our immune system, while practicing mindful breathing can be a great way to ground ourselves this fall. All of these practices can aid in balancing hormones and are a preferred way to release pent up energy that leads to high cortisol levels and stress.

- **October:** Daylight between 7:30am and 6:30pm
- **November:** Daylight between 7:10am and 4:50pm
- **December:** Daylight between 7:40am and 4:40pm

ASHLEY MICHAUD

FOOD GUIDE & RECIPES

Flu season is here and no amount of anti-bacterial gel or Vitamin C tablets will help. If your immune system / bacterial army is not prepared, a virus can get ahold of you too! Colds and flu can be terrible for you and all those concerned, not to mention, the average home spends at least 20% of their income on medicine and tissues. [4] [5]

    Again, nature provides us with the answer. The warmth of summer and dampness of autumn brings mushrooms and their immunity supporting benefits. All across the country, from woodland floors to decaying logs and meadows, we can find nature's beautiful solutions to any problem. In this food guide, I will also share with you my toddler-approved cold and flu season tincture.

    Here are our favorite fall foods, recipes, remedies, and tinctures for Elemental Growth, enjoy!

---

4   Davis, J. L. (2003, February 24). Cost of the Common Cold: $40 Billion. Retrieved from https://www.webmd.com/cold-and-flu/news/20030224/cost-of-common-cold-40-billion#1

5   Common cold costs $6-billion annually, researchers say. (2018, April 17). Retrieved from https://www.theglobeandmail.com/news/national/common-cold-costs-6-billion-annually-researchers-say/article1010986/

Breakfast - Sweet Toast

INGREDIENTS

1 sweet potato
1 avocado
1 tomato
½ cup sprouted microgreens or red sauerkraut

DIRECTIONS

- Slice sweet potato to fit in the toaster and toast 1-3 times.
- Top with avocado, tomatoes, sprouts/red sauerkraut.
- You may also eat these as is or add some hemp seeds and peanut butter for the kids to enjoy as well.

ASHLEY MICHAUD

AM Snack - Spiced Apples

INGREDIENTS

8-12 apples
Cinnamon (as desired)
Coconut oil (as desired)
Maple syrup (as desired)
Walnuts (as desired)

DIRECTIONS

- Heat oven to 350 degrees and core some apples.
- Next, place apples in a baking dish and stuff them with cinnamon, coconut oil, maple syrup and walnuts. Bake for 30 minutes.
- Enjoy warm as is or add a dollop of coconut or cashew cream with some cinnamon and walnuts.

Lunch – Super Spaghetti

INGREDIENTS

High protein noodles (Tastell is our go-to brand, you can find it on Amazon online)
1 can of organic whole tomatoes or fresh whole or cherry tomatoes
1 quart of mushrooms
3-4 celery stalks
Peppers (red, yellow, orange or green)
Carrots
2 onions
Himalayan sea salt to taste
Basil
Any other herbs and spices you desire

DIRECTIONS

- Find a high protein noodles like Tastell and cook according to instructions.
- For the sauce simmer whole tomatoes, or cherry tomatoes in water. Boost it with mushrooms, celery, peppers, garlic, carrots and onions.
- Add Himalayan salt, basil and other herbs that you find appealing.
- Mix the sauce with your pasta, add some mint or basil leaves and sprinkle some dairy free cheese on top and enjoy!

PM Snack – Seeded Fries

INGREDIENTS

White or red potatoes
1 sweet potato
Garlic powder
Salt to taste
Sesame seeds (white or black)
Hemp seeds

DIRECTIONS

- Boil some white or red potatoes and store them in the fridge.
- Slice them up to make fries along with one sweet potato.
- Coat with garlic, salt, sesame seeds (white/black) and hemp seeds and place on parchment paper lined baking tray.
- Bake in the oven at 350 degrees for at least 1 hour, flip and bake longer if you cut thick.
- Enjoy plain or with your favorite dipping sauce.

Supper – Foragers Pie

INGREDIENTS

1 cup sprouted green lentils
1 garlic bulb
1 onion
3 celery stalks
1 can of organic peas or frozen peas
2-3 fresh tomatoes
2-3 carrots
Thyme (as desired)
Oregano (as desired)
Himalyan sea salt to taste
Cauliflower or potatoes (for mash)

DIRECTIONS

- Cook sprouted green lentils in a vegetable broth.
- Add in garlic, onion, celery, peas, tomatoes, carrots, thyme, oregano and Himalayan sea salt.
- Fill ramekins with this mixture and top with mashed potatoes/cauliflower.
- Take it a step further and drizzle with natural ketchup.
- Bake at 350 degrees for 30 minutes.
- Enjoy plain or with some homemade ketchup or gravy.

Medicine – Elderberry Tincture

ELEMENTAL GROWTH TIP:

Elderberry is an age old natural remedy to common colds, cough, and flu and so much more. It is full of immune boosting properties and rich in flavonoids such as anthocyanins (which give it its deep purple color). It helps keep the immune system strong and keep viruses at bay.[6] Build up your immunity to the cold / flu or relieve your symptoms if you already have a cold / cough or the flu by trying our go-to recipe which is tried, true, and toddler-friendly.

Short on elderberries in your area? Echinacea also grows wild during this time of the year and is a great alternative. However, the taste did not pass the toddler taste test.

WHAT YOU NEED

1 quart elderberries
Apple cider vinegar

DIRECTIONS

- Fill a glass jar with elderberries and cover with apple cider vinegar.
- Let this sit in the cupboard for two weeks or up to one year.
- When you need it, strain the berries and add the tincture to a dropper bottle.

---

6 Elderberry / Elderflower Benefits & Information. (n.d.). Retrieved from https://www.indigo-herbs.co.uk/natural-health-guide/benefits/elderberry

Beauty – Rosehip Face Line

ELEMENTAL GROWTH TIP:

Roses are the definition of beauty and do wonders for the skin. Roses are simple to work with when making beauty remedies and can do everything from brightening the skin to more serious issues like acne and rosacea.

Rosehip Powder Cleanser

WHAT YOU NEED

¼ cup rolled oats
¼ cup bentonite clay
2 tablespoons activated charcoal
1 tablespoon rosehip oil

DIRECTIONS

- In a blender combine ¼ cup rolled oats, ¼ cup bentonite clay, 2 tablespoons activated charcoal and 1 tablespoons rosehip oil.
- Sprinkle on wet hands and rub into face. Rinse with warm water and a cloth.

ASHLEY MICHAUD *says*

Rosehip Micellar Water

WHAT YOU NEED

Rose petal clippings

DIRECTIONS

- Simmer rose clippings in the water on low heat for one hour with the lid on.
- Remove from heat and strain into a glass jar.
- Use this as a natural alternative to toner and high priced micellar waters.

Rosehip Face Cream

WHAT YOU NEED

¼ cup coconut oil
2 tablespoons beeswax
1 tablespoon almond oil
½ teaspoon rosehip oil
¼ teaspoon lavender essential oil
¼ cup aloe vera gel

DIRECTIONS

- Melt ¼ cup of coconut oil and 2 tablespoon of beeswax in a pot on medium heat.
- Remove from heat and add in 1 tablespoon of almond oil, ½ teaspoon of rosehip oil and ¼ teaspoon of lavender essential oil.
- Lastly, whisk/blend in ¼ cup aloe vera gel.
- This cream is good for face, body, kids, sunscreen and after sun lotion.

ASHLEY MICHAUD *eg*

MOVEMENT

Our metabolism shifts based on age, weight, activity level, body temperature, hormonal shifts, and our inner world balance. If we consume extra calories that our body cannot use, the body will store that energy (as body fat) for later use. Not all calories are created equal. Whole, nutrient-dense foods nourish and protect your body. The goal is to eat whole nutrient-dense food so our body will function optimally at the physical activity level that best suits your individual lifestyle and goals.

Regular exercise not only helps to prevent or manage a wide range of health problems and concerns, but it also helps improve hormonal and mental functions. The endocrine system regulates the production of hormones, which are chemicals that control our cellular functions. Hormones are responsible for both building new muscle and burning fat, so it is important to understand the hormones related to exercise and the functions they influence.

Any amount of activity is better than none at all, but to really get to the heart of it, consistency is key. Staying active stimulates various brain chemicals that may leave you feeling happier, more relaxed, and less anxious, hence giving us more focused energy to turn our passions into actions this fall. Exercise enhances many areas of life, in fact, research shows that the high achievers in the world move their bodies each day. Is exercise a part of your daily or weekly routine? Are you a newbie, runner, gym junkie, or at-home yoga guru? Share with us in the group: https://www.facebook.com/groups/elementalgrowth/

If you don't have a regular routine in place, push yourself to try something physically active each day this month. Get a free two-week pass at your local gym, sign-up for a class or find a yoga routine like Yoga With Adriene, Boho Beautiful or Banana Blondie 108 on YouTube.

TOP TIPS FOR CREATING YOUR FITNESS REGIMENT

Cardio – Aim for 150 minutes per week (or thirty minutes, five days per week). It is recommended that you make this activity part of your schedule.

Strength training – Aim for two strength training workouts each week. Make sure that they target all the major muscle groups, including your abs, arms, back, chest, hips, legs, and shoulders.

Personal trainer – A trainer teaches effective workout strategies to keep us interested and seeing results. Having a personal trainer who will offer ideas and advice about how to maximize our results can really help even if its virtual.

Drink lots of water – If you have been exercising, then you will need to drink more water to replace the water that your body has lost.

And don't forget to cut down on alcohol and smoking – Alcohol adds empty calories to your diet and both alcohol consumption and smoking also cause dehydration, fatigue, and other health problems.

CHECK-IN ACTIVITY

As your relationship with nature grows you will find that elimination is not a gross word, rather it is a naturally occurring process in the ebb and flow of Mother Nature. We discover that when we let go, we open ourselves for renewal. We take 23,040 breaths a day, 8,409,600 a year making us an expert in this process already. Our body has everything it needs to heal itself and the ability to function without us even being conscious. As we take a moment to appreciate that, take a deep breath in through your nose filling your lungs and belly, hold this tight feeling for a minute and release everything holding you back from freedom.

FALL ELIMINATION PROTOCOL

Body - Element Earth: This is where all our memories are stored. The way we process things everyday depends on being able to recall, create, and develop memories. Our blood, brain, hormones, muscles, every cell in our body relies on what we expose it to. This is a great time for a guided elimination diet, cleanse, detox or fast.

Breath - Element Air: Get out into nature, a forest or beach where the air is fresh. If the option is available to you, plan a trip to the country to eliminate toxins and renew every cell in your body.

Spirit - Element Fire: Have a fire ceremony alone or with some friends. Write down all the things you wish to release into the universe from past ideas and beliefs to dreams for the future - let it all go by burning your papers. If your paper does not burn the first time, consider if there is something you are still hanging onto.

Intuition - Element Water: This is all about how we flow in life, trust your intuition and allow that little voice to become stronger and speak its desires. This is a great time to have a good cry, join a gym, have a steam, wash your windows, visit a waterfall or enjoy a herbal bath.

ELIMINATION DIET

Do you experience skin issues, leaky gut, bloating, swollen lymph glands, indigestion, autoimmune disease, or brain fog? Then this is for you. An elimination diet involves removing specific foods that may be causing allergic reactions or signs of intolerance. Common allergens include soy, dairy, eggs, fish, shellfish, caffeine, gluten, and nuts. It may take anywhere from 7 days to 6 months for any particular allergen to be completely removed by the body. Not everyone is allergic to these common allergens either - maybe you are immune to everything in your environment or allergic to something less common like lavender or carrots which are not on the list.

Soy: tingling in the mouth, hives; itching; or itchy, scaly skin (eczema), swelling of the lips, face, tongue and throat, or other body parts, wheezing, a runny nose or breathing difficulty, abdominal pain, diarrhea, nausea or vomiting, skin redness (flushing).

Dairy: abdominal cramps, loose stools, which may contain blood, diarrhea. coughing or wheezing, runny nose, watery eyes, itchy milk allergy rash on the skin, commonly found around the mouth, colic (in babies).

Eggs: skin inflammation or hives, nasal congestion, runny nose and sneezing (allergic rhinitis), digestive symptoms, such as cramps, nausea and vomiting, asthma signs and symptoms such as coughing, wheezing, chest tightness or shortness of breath.

Fish / shellfish: tingling in the mouth, abdominal pain, nausea, diarrhea, or vomiting, congestion, trouble breathing, or wheezing, skin reactions including itching, hives, or eczema, swelling of the face, lips, tongue, throat, ears, fingers, or hands, lightheadedness, dizziness, or fainting.

Caffeine: skin problems such as hives, eczema, rashes, acne, severe itching, headaches or migraines, anxiety and panic attacks, lack of focus, swelling of the tongue, glands or throat, heart racing or palpitations, angry and irritable mood, fatigue.

Gluten/Wheat: digestive issues such as gas, bloating, diarrhea or constipation, Keratosis Pilaris, (also known as "chicken skin" on the back of your arms), fatigue, brain fog or feeling tired after eating a meal that contains gluten, diagnosis of an autoimmune disease such as Hashimoto's thyroiditis, rheumatoid arthritis, ulcerative colitis, lupus, psoriasis, scleroderma or multiple sclerosis, neurologic symptoms such as dizziness or feeling of being off balance, hormone imbalances such as premenstrual syndrome (PMS), polycystic ovarian syndrome (PCOS) or unexplained infertility, migraine headaches, diagnosis of chronic fatigue or fibromyalgia, inflammation, swelling or pain in our joints such as fingers, knees or hips, mood issues such as anxiety, depression, mood swings and attention deficit disorder (ADD).

Nuts: abdominal pain, cramps, nausea and vomiting, diarrhea, difficulty swallowing, itching of the mouth, throat, eyes, skin or any other area, nasal congestion or a runny nose, nausea, shortness of breath, anaphylaxis.

You may have one or more of these symptoms or none at all as foods affect each person differently - "One man's food is another man's poison." The only way to be sure is to experiment for yourself. Although most doctors see this as harmless these days and some are even recommending it to their clients now as an alternative to blood testing and before prescribing medications, if you have any serious health issues, I do recommend that you speak with your doctor before starting this diet just to be safe. Our method at Elemental Growth is to ask yourself which you think maybe a trigger and start there. Rank them in order and begin eliminating them one at a time and tracking your results in a food journal or app. Take my client, Shannon, for example:

Shannon, 42 years old | Spiritual Entrepreneur

Shannon suspected that she may have a gluten sensitivity because of a recent hormonal diagnosis she received. Shannon listed wheat / gluten as her number one suspect so we created a two-week gluten-free menu for her to fol-

low along with some tips for convenience and last minute snacks. By the end of two weeks, we slowly introduced gluten back into her diet and she noticed that she immediately felt and looked bloated. Because Shannon had already invested two-weeks into a gluten-free lifestyle she felt comfortable to continue exploring gluten-free cooking and shopping methods.

For Shannon, we were able to figure things out quickly but for you, it may take longer. You may have to go through the whole list of top allergens, taking notes along the way but there is always a light at the end of the tunnel and so many options available to us today from requisitioned blood and allergy testing to online/at-home kits. The most important takeaway here though is that you are taking your health into your own hands, tuning into what your body is telling you, and healing yourself!

This is what the experts don't want you to know: You hold all the power, you are the one responsible for the healing, you are responsible for your quality of life, health and happiness. You are the healer, the guru, and divine. Get back to the basics by following these steps:

- Find out what your unique body needs to function optimally.
- Find out what is toxic to your body and any sensitivities you may have.
- Give your body what it needs to thrive at least 90% of the time.
- Avoid the things that dim your light or make you feel regretful.
- Rise up and experience Elemental Growth.

CHAPTER 5
True Alchemy (Aether)

"The more you are in harmony with nature, the more likely you are to be in the right place at the right time all of the time."
– Joshua Rosenthal

Throughout this book, we focused on the first four elements that are considered to make up the world in which we live—Earth, Air, Fire, and Water. Each element evokes an emotional response that stimulates our minds, calms our nerves, and enriches our lives. These four elements also represent the first four chakras or what is known as the lower triangle chakras.

The best way to understand how vital these elements are is to connect with them in nature, so get your hands dirty in the garden, let the sun penetrate your eyes and skin, stay well hydrated and make time for activities that light you up.

- **Root Chakra (Earth):** associated with our lower body, spine, and adrenal glands; responds to instinct and survival, symbolizes our food, soil, and roots. Read more: https://elementalgrowth.org/root-chakra-muladhara-root-support/
- **Sacral Chakra (Water):** associated with the ovaries and testes, symbolizes our emotions and creativity. Read more: https://elementalgrowth.org/2nd-chakra-svadhishthana-oness-own/
- **Solar Plexus Chakra (Fire):** associated with the liver,

pancreas, and gallbladder; responsible for empowerment and transformation. Read more: https://elementalgrowth.org/3rd-chakra-solar-plexus-manipura/

- **Heart Chakra (Air):** associated with our heart and thymus; highlights our ability to love and express gratitude. Read more: https://elementalgrowth.org/4th-chakra-heart-anahata/

Our higher chakras such as the throat, third eye, and crown are represented by the element Aether - the god particle, quintessence, or dark matter. This is the element which fills all the rest. This is the life force energy and universal consciousness which we all have the opportunity to tap into.

- **Throat Chakra:** associated with the thyroid, our expression, truth, and authenticity.
- **Third Eye Chakra:** associated with the pituitary gland, hormone regulation, wisdom, and intuition.
- **Crown Chakra:** associated with the pineal gland, the dream world, interconnection, and spirituality.

CHAKRA MAPPING

Signs of unease often show up in our energetic field first. When we ignore the signs our body sends us, it then tends to cluster physical symptoms in a certain region of the body. In nutrition school, we call this the law of geographic proximity and in Reiki, we refer to it as a blockage in one or more of your chakras. This will continue to disrupt your natural "flow" until that area is cleared and aligned.

When you feel symptoms in an area of your body or notice that your energy and emotions are out of balance, listen and allow your body to reveal a pattern or an area where an ailment is focused. What you may have thought was causing a problem may really only be a side effect of the root cause. Take my client, Charlotte, for example:

Charlotte, 28 years old | Stay-at-home-mom

Charlotte came to me looking for natural alternatives to medication. She was irritable, gaining belly fat, and ready to give up on life—everything bad was always happening to her. During one of our sessions, I asked Charlotte if she would be open to a chakra mapping exercise, she agreed and what we found, changed her entire life around.
We found that most of Charlotte's pain and symptoms were coming from her gut—the area of the solar-plexus chakra. As we dug deeper, we found some patterns that often get overlooked. Charlotte experienced low self-esteem, a victim mindset, and was drinking almost every night. Was this Charlotte?

Short answer: no! These are all symptoms of the root problem. Once we identified where the issues were stemming from, Charlotte and I began experimenting with different practices to help unblock the energy stored in this chakra so her natural energies could flow once again.

We started with swapping out Charlotte's morning coffee with dandelion root and after supper drink with kombucha (fermented tea that is beneficial for maintaining good gut flora). We also added in some other yellow foods like sauerkraut, lemon water, quinoa, and tropical fried rice dishes. We developed a core-based workout routine that Charlotte could commit to and explored her fears about fitting-in that stemmed from early childhood beliefs—beliefs that no longer benefited her survival and hindered her ability to shine.

Today Charlotte has quit many bad habits and evaluated her belief system. She continues to eat nutrient-dense food as a way to embrace her will-power. Charlotte took responsibility for her life and now makes decisions based on what feels right for her, fearless of what others may say.

Charlotte expressed that as the anger lifted post detox, her digestive issues improved, her mind got clearer, her sleep became more regular, and the extra weight that bothered her just melted away.

Are one or more of your energy centers blocked? Similar to Charlotte, some of your symptoms may be physical, while others may be emotional or energetic. Explore all of them and see what patterns arise.

In the space below, fill in any ailments or uneasy feelings coming from the associated locations. Dis-ease tends to show up in our energy field first. When we're having physical issues, this may be due to the fact that our body is communicating what we have neglected to observe within ourselves. Mark the areas where symptoms occur.

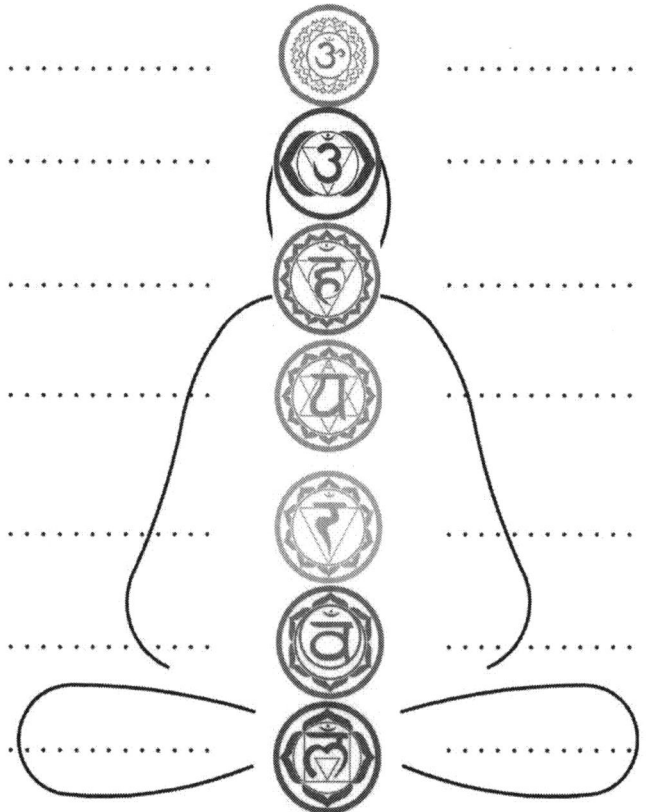

ASHLEY MICHAUD

- Do you notice any patterns?

  _____
  _____
  _____

- What do you suspect is the root cause?

  _____
  _____
  _____

- Where in your body do you feel symptoms the most?

  _____
  _____
  _____

- How might you address the root cause?

  _____
  _____
  _____

- Anything else that you feel as you scan your body for symptoms and patterns?

  _____
  _____
  _____

CREATE YOUR OWN TRADITIONS

Tradition by definition is a family ritual—an activity you purposefully repeat together as a family. We continue to repeat our parents' traditions but want to stress the value of renewing them with new spirit and intention.

Step 1 - Find a purpose, significant date or rite of passage. Ask yourself: "What do I hope my family and I will get out of it?"

Step 2 - Once you know your purpose, personalize your tradition. This could mean preparing a special meal, game, activity or something else.

Step 3 - As opportunities present themselves, talk to your family about what they liked and didn't like. Get creative, compromise, integrate in new traditions.

Step 4 - Focus your energies on creating your own traditions that are unique to your new family as you grow. Traditions that work when you are single will change once you have children, and as your children get older, these traditions may change again.

Step 5 - Family traditions are one of those areas where quality beats quantity every time. Take things slow making little tweaks each time. Remember to enjoy the process.

SAMPLE TRADITIONS

Birthdays

- Give the gift of a new experience.
- Share a special meal with loved ones.
- Make a wish for the new year to come.

Winter Tradition: Winter Solstice, December 21st

- Celebrate Christmas dinner and gift exchange with extended family / friends.

- Write out New Year's resolutions, plan action steps and set-up new agenda.
- Invite friends out for a nature hike and fire ceremony.

Spring Tradition: Spring Equinox, March 20
- Host a swap party with my friends to purge all our clutter / unnecessary items.
- Commit to a cleanse or fasting program to reset the body.
- Take a nature hike and forage for fiddleheads and morel mushrooms.

Summer Tradition: Summer Solstice, June 21
- Do something you have always wanted to do for no other reason.
- Add something new to the garden and share cuttings with others.
- Host a BBQ and dance under the midnight moon.

Fall Tradition: Fall Equinox, September 23
- Invite friends and family to a harvest feast and dance.
- Practice an elimination diet for at least two weeks.
- Purge old ideas, beliefs, plans, and close out the year.

MOON CYCLES AND REGULATING OUR HORMONE CYCLE FOR WOMEN

Are you a victim of irregular menstruation? In the beginning, a woman's menstrual cycle would sync up with the moon. On the new moon, when the sky is dark, women would come together in space to tap into their inner voice and creativity. During the full moon, women would ovulate and be at their sexual peak. This has changed much over the generations, but we still see glimpses of it today when we sync up our cycles with other women close to us.

Get your cycle back on track:

Step 1 - I stabilize my blood sugar by:

_____

_____

Step 2 - I nurture my adrenals by:

_____

_____

Step 3 - I support my organs of elimination by:

_____

_____

Step 4 - I am training my menstrual cycle by:

_____

_____

Step 5 - I am engaging my feminine energy by:

_____

_____

FOR MEN

Are you a victim of irregular mood swings & cravings? PubMed published an article that suggests that men in serious relationships with women often sync up with the woman's moon cycle by shifting their androgen levels weekly so that the couple will have a better chance to reproduce come the full moon. This is a biological response that most men are not aware of. In addition, bachelors likely will not experience these same shifts. [7]

Get your cycle back on track:

Step 1 - I stabilize my blood sugar by:

_____

_____

Step 2 - I nurture my adrenals by:

_____

_____

Step 3 - I support my organs of elimination by:

_____

_____

Step 4 - I am training my muscles by:

_____

_____

Step 5 - I am engaging my masculine energy by:

_____

_____

---

7   Monthly Patterns of Testosterone and Behavior in Prospective Fathers. (2002, September 28). Retrieved from https://www.sciencedirect.com/science/article/pii/S0018506X02918155?via=ihub

Take my client, Tristan, for example:

Tristan, 33 years old | Business Owner, Film & Media

When Tristan first came to me, he was having trouble losing weight and went back and forth between the vegetarian and the standard american diet (SAD). Within two weeks, Tristan was tuning into his moon cycles by keeping his version of a food journal. Tristan has lost those last ten pounds and to sustain his muscle definition and positive attitude, he continues to follow these steps.

To stabilize Tristan's blood sugar, we took a shopping tour at a store in his local community and checked out some restaurants that he could make a quick stop at if he is ever in a rush for food or has unexpected company. We identified hidden sugars on labels and had his questions answered about specific foods.

Tristan nurtures his adrenals by reducing blue light at night, he identified that the blue light from his TV and video games was interfering with his sleep cycles and in return his hormones. He now supports his organs of elimination by including fibrous fruits and vegetables into his diet. Tristan also enjoys fresh cilantro which is a great detoxifying herb.

Tristan trains his muscles by developing new skills, strength training, and playing with his daughter. Tristan has found that the best way for him to engage his masculine energy is by becoming self-sustainable and building his own passion based business from the ground up. Tristan also tunes into the moon cycles frequently and looks to leaders like the late Alan Watts for guidance.

ASHLEY MICHAUD

OVERVIEW OF THE FEMALE HORMONE CYCLE

NEW MOON	FIRST QUARTER
- Menstruation Phase - Lasts 3-7 days - Progesterone drops - Estrogen peaks, then drops - May experience fatigue, cramping or cravings - Communication between right / left brain peaks - This is the time to nurture your gut & intuition - Journal or create vision boards - Eat low glycemic, high water fruits / veggies - Increase iron & zinc intake through food like beans & sea veggies or supplements - Practice restorative type yoga	- Follicular phase - Lasts 7-10 days - FSH and Estrogen increase - May feel restless, creative & upbeat - This is a good time to mastermind, and say yes to events - Eat fresh vibrant, light foods - Experiment with a new activity / fitness routine - Step outside your comfort zone
FULL MOON	**THIRD QUARTER**
- Ovulatory phase - Lasts 3-4 days - FSH, Luteinizing and Estrogen increase - Testosterone drops - May experience discharge - Fertility peaks - This is a good time to connect - You may become more magnetic - Your communication skills may increase - Fill up on fiber-rich veggies / fruit - Introduce a high impact workout in a group setting	- Luteal phase - Lasts 10-14 days - Progesterone and Estrogen increase - FSH and Lutein decrease - Your energy may naturally decline - Your awareness, attention, focus may increase - This is time for nesting, cleaning and shopping - Stay in and do some batch cooking - Focus on self-care like a bath, book or movie - Increase B vitamins, calcium, magnesium and fiber - Eat leafy greens and baked veggies to curb sugar cravings - Eat complex carbs - curb mood swings - Take a walk or practice yoga at home

* Adapted from Alisa Vitti's *Woman Code: Perfect Your Cycle, Amplify Your Fertility, Supercharge Your Sex Drive, And Become A Power Source.*

CIRCADIAN RHYTHM

MORNING ROUTINE CHECKLIST
- Sunlight & hydrate
- Morning movement
- Breath & meditation
- Enjoy breakfast
- Morning pages

GRATITUDES
I'm grateful for _____
I'm grateful for _____
I'm grateful for _____

GOALS
Today, I am _____
Today, I am _____
Today, I am _____

AFFIRMATIONS
Just for today, I _____
Just for today, I _____
Just for today, I _____

ASHLEY MICHAUD *eg*

ELEMENTAL RHYTHM

NIGHT ROUTINE CHECKLIST

- Finish eating by 8pm
- Wash the day away
- Tomorrow's to-do's
- Evening prayer / reflection
- Get horizontal, call in those zzzz's by 10pm

LOVE

Today, I loved _____

Today, I loved _____

Today, I loved _____

LESSONS

Today, I learned _____

Today, I learned _____

Today, I learned _____

TOMORROW'S TO-DO'S

Tomorrow, I will _____

Tomorrow, I will _____

Tomorrow, I will _____

FOOD GUIDE

EAT THE RAINBOW

The color of your food can tell you a lot about its nutritional value, plus eating a variety of colors is a trusted method to get as many of those vitamins and minerals as possible. For most people, as long as you eat a well-rounded, balanced diet, you'll get the nutrients you need, in a form that your body can use. Eating the rainbow will also ensure that you get a diversity of gut bacteria which is interconnected with all other body functions.

Most Americans aren't getting the range of colorful foods they need. According to a 2009 phytonutrients report (based on data from the National Health and Nutrition Examination Surveys), eight out of ten people in the U.S are falling short in virtually every color category of phytonutrients. Based on the report:

- 78% of Americans are falling short in red phytonutrients.
- 79% of Americans are falling short in yellow and orange phytonutrients.
- 69% of Americans are falling short in green phytonutrients.
- 88% of Americans are falling short in purple and blue phytonutrients.
- 86% of Americans are falling short in white phytonutrients.

Our bodies benefit from variety, we need a rainbow of nutrients and colors. In fact, the variety of vitamins, minerals, antioxidants, and phytochemicals in fruits and vegetables have enormous healing powers. Eating a diversity of colorful foods can be an easy way to get a complete range of vitamins and minerals your body needs to thrive.

As you continue to read on, you will learn the essentials of each chakra and how eating the rainbow will help you reach your health and wellness goals.[8]

Eating new things, and experimenting with different foods is essential to getting into healthy habits like cooking at home. Everyday, learn a bit more about the nutritional value of the foods you want to try, and how they compare to the things you already eat and you may find that change comes naturally.

When we include each of the seven colors each day we provide nourishing fuel to our body. Most times you can even clear and balance your chakras to heal physical symptoms before they even develop. That is one of the best things about chakra therapies, you can address issues before they manifest in your body.

Whether you want to lose weight, nourish your chakras or increase your energy levels, incorporating foods from all the colors of the rainbow will help you achieve balance, so you look and feel your best.

Like anything else, all foods hold a vibration. For example, pesticides, animal products, and processed foods hold lower vibrations, whereas plants have higher vibrations. An example is of a low vibration foods is taking a bite out of a burger that came from a fearful creature and then developing stress and tension caused by fear yourself. Just as after eating processed foods, you may feel sluggish or experience lower vibrational energies including worry, which can affect the root chakra and others. Start by avoiding certain foods like conventionally farmed meat and dairy because the animals are usually stressed-out, sick, and unhappy. You are what you eat, so consume foods that will nourish you, give you vitality, and help your life force stay vibrant!

---

8   Choosing Foods by Color? - Ask Dr. Weil. (2016, December 01). Retrieved from https://www.drweil.com/diet-nutrition/nutrition/choosing-foods-by-color/

This is a common belief amongst yogis, as it is thought that the energetic imprint left on the meat from an animal can be transferred when consumed. In Native American tradition, we are to give thanks after every kill, and nothing would go to waste. Once you've awakened this awareness, I encourage you to listen to your body after you eat certain foods, and ask yourself: *How does this make me feel? Or what is it my body is really craving?*

We all go through moments when we feel lazy, unconfident, unsuccessful, fatigued, depressed, anxious, frustrated, emotional, burnt out, etc. But what if there was a way to overcome these feelings free of addictive tendencies, pharmaceuticals, or therapy so that we could get back to our awesome, motivated, rockin' selves?

BUILD YOUR MENU - EATING FOR YOUR CHAKRAS

FOUR PRINCIPLES

1. Each food, according to its outer color, which is its reflecting surface, can be related to the specific color and energy of a particular chakra.
2. Different-color foods are specific for energizing, balancing, and healing their corresponding color-related chakras.
3. Each color food energizes, cleanses, builds, heals, and rebalances the glands, organs, and nerve centers associated with its color related chakra.
4. The purpose of the Rainbow Diet is to help balance, on a regular daily cycle, each individual chakra, its associated organs, glands, and nerve plexus, and the chakra system as a whole.

The color of a food is its signature. As we become sensitive to nature's efforts to communicate to us through her beautiful colors, shapes, markings and other we begin to develop a sensitivity to the particular food we are drawn to on a specific day as a key to what food energy and nutrients we need to balance our body.

ROOT CHAKRA/MULADHARA

- **Element:** earth
- **Body:** adrenal glands, corresponds to instinct and survival.
- **Balanced:** safe, secure, grounded
- **Unbalanced:** joints, hips, knees, thighs, lower back, feet, feelings of insecurity, unsafe, survivor, fight or flight
- **Nutrition:** bright red foods from the earth, food grown with deep roots or on a vine, red herbal teas
- **Practice:** walk barefoot, beach yoga
- **Mantra:** I am establishing roots by learning to forgive my caregivers from early childhood. I am safe safe, secure, and my basic needs are being met on a daily basis. I am the hero of my own story.

SACRAL CHAKRA/SVADHISTHANA

- **Element:** water
- **Body:** ovaries and testes, emotions and creativity
- **Balanced:** healthy relationships, pleasure, joy, balance, harmony, creating, abundance
- **Unbalanced:** addictions, negative self-image, hormone imbalance, infertility, cravings
- **Nutrition:** earth and trace minerals, mushrooms, water, orange foods, orange spices and teas
- **Practice:** daily affirmations, yoga, swimming, hiking, massage

- **Mantra:** I am expressing my creativity and pursuing my passions. I am nurturing my intuition and my relationships that thrive.

SOLAR PLEXUS/MANIPURA

- **Element:** fire
- **Body:** pancreas, empowerment and transformation
- **Balanced:** worthy, progress, warmth, comfort, healthy boundaries, self-worth, inner power, energy, gut / intuition, trust, intimacy, eye contact
- **Unbalanced:** unbalanced cortisol and insulin levels, powerless, victim, irregular sleep patterns, stress, adrenal fatigue, poor listening habits, acidic body, victim
- **Nutrition:** fermented foods, yellow vegetables, healthy fats and yellow herbal teas
- **Practice:** meditation, outdoor activities, breathwork, yogic twists and ab work
- **Mantra:** I am authentic and intuitive. I am tuned in and manifesting my goals.

HEART CHAKRA/ANAHATA

- **Element:** air
- **Body:** heart and thymus, love and gratitude
- **Balanced:** love, open, calm, forgiveness, unity, letting go to be present
- **Unbalanced:** isolation, heart / circulation issues, fear, panic, tension, lungs, oxygen
- **Nutrition:** nutrient-rich vegetables, leafy greens, seaweed, alkalizing fruit, healthy fats, raw nuts, green vegetables, aloe juice and water
- **Practice:** breathing techniques, good posture, roll-

ing shoulders back, hearth openers, walks, hikes and gardening
- **Mantra:** I am full of joy, compassion, and love, not only for others but myself. I am letting go of the past and forgiving everybody for everything and establishing my own self-worth.

THROAT CHAKRA/VISHUDDHA

- **Element:** ether
- **Body:** thyroid, truth and authenticity
- **Balanced:** truth, communication, warmth, innovative ideas
- **Unbalanced:** gland and thyroid issues, hormonal imbalance, unable to speak your truth
- **Nutrition:** blue foods and herbal teas, nutrition from all elements
- **Practice:** speaking truthfully (in person, journal or visualization) and getting things off of your chest
- **Mantra:** I am focusing my energy on true expression, intuition, integrity, honesty, and openness.

THIRD EYE CHAKRA/AJNA

- **Element:** light
- **Body:** pituitary gland, eyes, brain, ears, wisdom and intuition
- **Balanced:** connection, oneness, synchronicity, psychic ability, premonitions, visions
- **Unbalanced:** neurosis, headaches, self-sacrifice, confusion, mental illness
- **Nutrition:** sprouted nuts, metal detox, purple foods, cruciferous vegetables, wild meat/fish

- **Practice:** meditation, yoga, long stretches, hiking, Tai Chi, travel
- **Mantra:** I am nurturing my intuition, my ability to plan and each of my senses. I am guided, clear and part of the solution.

CROWN CHAKRA/SAHASRARA

- **Element:** universal consciousness
- **Body:** pineal gland, nervous system, interconnection and spirituality
- **Balanced:** vibrant, glowing, supported, flow, higher intelligence, manifestation, mindful
- **Unbalanced:** neuroses, migraines, nerves, joints, loneliness, unsupported, delusional
- **Nutrition:** water, natural salt, cleansing herbs, seeds, vegetable broth, garlic, miso, mushrooms and naturally white & violet food/tea
- **Practice:** positive thoughts and visualizations, asking for help, gratitude exercises
- **Mantra:** I am nourished by love and my strong connection to the divine. I am engaging in spirit-lifting activities and mediation.

It's time to create your rainbow menu: Experiment with recipes that where you can include every color. Get social by using #ElementalGrowth or tagging us at @IamElementalGrowth so we can find and support you.

ASHLEY MICHAUD
PLAN YOUR MEALS

BREAKFAST	
AM SNACK	
LUNCH	
PM SNACK	
SUPPER	

SHOPPING LIST

- _____   _____
- _____   _____
- _____   _____
- _____   _____
- _____   _____

MOVEMENT
CREATE YOUR FITNESS PLAN

Stress, hard work, overthinking, and emotional and mental baggage can all create tension in the body, which can lead to chronic aches, tightness, and constipation. Many people try to alleviate these symptoms with alcohol and sugar, which can turn unease into disease in no time. Exercise is a rewarding and necessary way to release this physical tension.

The key is finding the types of exercise you enjoy most so that you can easily build them into your routine and stay committed to long term progress.

Things to consider:

- What will get you moving?
- What did you enjoy doing as a kid?
- How are you feeling in your body?
- Are you introverted or a social butterfly?
- Do you enjoy competition?
- What time of the day is best for you?
- Where is convenient?
- What atmosphere are you looking for?
- What little things can you start including?
- Do you require a friend / trainer to keep you accountable?

ASHLEY MICHAUD *eyes*

TRACK YOUR FITNESS

Keeping track of your exercise routine allows you to start out slowly and make small adjustments as you progress. Keep you goals simple at first—showing up everyday no matter how busy you are or mood you are in will provide you with a strong foundation. Tracking your "actual" exercise will help you set realistic goals.

DATE & TIME	TYPE	FOOD	MOOD	GOAL
SUNDAY				
MONDAY				
TUESDAY				
WEDNESDAY				
THURSDAY				
FRIDAY				
SATURDAY				

Get social by using #ElementalGrowth or tagging us at @IamElementalGrowth so we can find and support you.

REVIEWING YOUR WEEK

At the end of each week review your progress by asking yourself:

- How did I impact my energy levels?
  _____
  _____

- When did I feel my best?
  _____
  _____

- How was my quality of sleep?
  _____
  _____

- How did my workouts impact my eating habits?
  _____
  _____

- How did food, exercise, and sleep impact my mood?
  _____
  _____

- Anything else that you notice or feel:
  _____
  _____

ASHLEY MICHAUD

CHECK-IN ACTIVITIES

GET THROUGH TO THE REAL YOU

To live your best life, you must be living authentically and to do that, you must get really clear on who you are, where you are going, what you value, and what you're passionate about. Use the following prompts to help you start tapping into your most authentic self.

- My proudest accomplishment so far in my life is:
  _____

- The scariest thing I've ever overcome is:
  _____

- Something I don't like to tell people about myself is:
  _____

- Something I never thought I could ever accomplish is:
  _____

- The most vulnerable time in my life was:
  _____

- What I am most afraid of is:
  _____

- What I love most about myself is:
  _____

- What I need to work on most about myself is:
  _____

- What I need to accept about myself is:
  _____

Now let's try an activity that will align you with your goal, values, passions and actions over a 1 month period.
For example, I make time on the 9th of each month (my birthday) to do this activity. Affirmations build good habits when developed with positive intentions and as you begin manifesting one, you'll end up manifesting more of them simultaneously!

Start by choosing 1-3 sacred words from the list that want to improve on. When you are done turn them into empowerment affirmations that you can use daily for 30 days or more. Choose one day each month when you can revisit this list.

SACRED WORDS

- _____
- _____
- _____
- _____
- _____

EMPOWERING AFFIRMATIONS

- _____
- _____
- _____
- _____
- _____

ASHLEY MICHAUD *eyes*

SELF-INQUIRY

- Were you surprised by anything that others noticed about you? Or that you noticed about yourself?

  _____
  _____
  _____

- Do you tend to show or hide more of yourself?

  _____
  _____
  _____

- What are the parts of yourself that you hide away from the world? Why might you be doing this?

  _____
  _____
  _____

- Are there characteristics of any aspect of your persona that don't currently serve you? How can you work on releasing them?

  _____
  _____
  _____

- Are there undeveloped aspects of yourself - characteristics that you'd like to cultivate? If so, how could you begin to do this?

  _____
  _____
  _____

SACRED WORDS OF EMPOWERMENT

A. Able, Accepting, Adaptable, Aces, Abundant, Authentic.

B. Bold, Brave, Beautiful, Bountiful.

C. Calm, Caring, Cheerful, Clever, Confident, Courteous, Charismatic, Creative.

D. Dependable, Dignified, Diligent.

E. Empathetic, Energetic, Extraverted.

F. Friendly, Fortitude, Funny, Fit, Fabulous.

G. Giving, Generous, Good, Grateful.

H. Happy, Helpful, Honest, Humorous.

I. Idealistic, Independent, Ingenious, Intelligent.

J. Justice, Joyful.

K. Kind, Knowledgable.

L. Logical, Loving, Loyal.

M. Mature, Modest, Magic, Monogamous .

O. Observant, Organized, Orderliness, Open-Minded, Original.

P. Patient, Powerful, Proud, Prudence, Passionate, Positive, Peaceful, Pure, Perseverance.

Q. Quiet, Quick.

R. Reflective, Relaxed, Religious, Responsive, Responsible, Respectful, Ridiculous

S. Self-assertive, Sensible, Silly, Spontaneous, Sympathetic, Serving, Strong, Sincere.

T. Trustworthy, Temperance, Tolerance, Tactful, Tender.

W. Warm, Wise, Witty, Wild.

ASHLEY MICHAUD *eys*

RECIPE SHARE

SPICED PEAR BAKE: In a bowl mix 2 cups of oats, 1 can coconut milk, 2 tablespoons melted coconut oil, ¼ cup maple syrup, 1 teaspoon baking powder, 1 teaspoon cinnamon, 1 teaspoon ginger, 1 teaspoon nutmeg, 2 teaspoons vanilla extract. Add to cast iron skillet or deep dish pie pan. Garnish with 2-3 thinly sliced pears, ½ cup chopped walnuts and a dash of salt. Bake at 350 degrees for 40 minutes.

PB & J CREPES: 2 cups gluten-free flour, 2 cups plant-based milk (or water), 2 mashed bananas, salt and cinnamon (optional).

PEANUT BUTTER: Blend roasted, unsalted peanuts until desired texture, you can add other nuts seeds, cocoa, or natural sweeteners as you desire but from my experience simply is best.

CHIA SEED JAM: Blend 2 cups of chopped fruit, 1 tbsp. lemon juice and 1 tablespoon. maple syrup, and 2 tablespoons chia seeds. Chill overnight. This recipe lasts 1 week in the fridge.

AVOCADO BOATS: Cut an avocado in half lengthwise and remove the core, fill the avocado with a filling of your choice and enjoy this brain boosting breakfast.

BERRIES & CHOCOLATE DRIZZLE AVO BOAT: Fill avocadoboat with your favorite berries and drizzle with dark chocolate (cocoa paste/powder, coconut oil, agave, vanilla).

AVO BOAT WITH CHICKPEA MASH: Mash chickpeas and mix in some celery, green onion, red pepper, garlic powder and mustard. Fill boat with mixture and top with red sauerkraut (red cabbage in a salt water brine).

SWEET TOAST: Slice a sweet potato to fit in the toaster and toast 1-3 times. Top with avocado, tomatoes, sprouts/red sauerkraut. You may also eat these as it or for the kids add peanut butter and hemp seeds.

CINASIM SMOOTHIE: Blend persimmons, apples, frozen bananas, cinnamon, chia/hemp seeds, and plant-based milk and maca root (optional).

STRAWBERRY AID: Blend lemon, maple syrup, frozen strawberries and bananas.

HULK BOWLS: Blend up two frozen banana with 1 tablespoon spirulina. Take it a step further and top it with a blackberry chia jam (1 cup mashed berries, ¼ cup chia seeds and honey to taste), add a sprinkle with hemp seeds and enjoy - we call this one space cream.

SPICED APPLES: Heat oven to 300 degrees and core some apples. Place them in a baking dish and stuff them with cinnamon, coconut oil, maple syrup and walnuts. Bake for thirty minutes.

HARVEST SANDWICH: Mix crushed walnuts with hummus and spread onto toast or wrap. Add field greens and sliced pear. Good on most bread, wraps or buns. We get the gluten-free and vegan bagels from O'doughs.

HUMMUS: Blend 1 can chickpeas, ¼ cup tahini, cumin, salt, garlic, and lemon to taste.

RAINBOW KALE SALAD: Chop and massage kale with olive oil and Himalayan sea salt. Add red onion, carrot, yellow peppers, broccoli, raisins, purple garlic, cooked rice/quinoa, pumpkin seeds, flax seeds and sunflower seeds.

CREAMY AVO SALAD DRESSING: Mix 1 mashed avocado, Himalayan sea salt, apple cider vinegar and maple syrup. Garnish with purple sauerkraut.

SUMMER LOVE SALAD: Combine quinoa, wild rice, kale, persulane, blueberries, concord grapes, sunflower seeds, walnuts, and drizzle with honey and balsamic vinegar.

SUPER SPAGHETTI: Find a high protein noodles like Tastell and cook according to instructions. For the sauce simmer whole tomatoes, or cherry tomatoes in water. Boost it with mushrooms, celery, peppers, garlic, carrots, and onions. Add Himalayan salt, basil, and other herbs that you find appealing.

RAINBOW HASH: Always cook potatoes in a batch the night before and chill to create resistant starch the kind that is low on the glycemic index. Cube or grate these potatoes, then fry them up with red cabbage, onions, broccoli, salt, and Dijon mustard.

BEET CHIPS: Slice thinly using a processor or mandoline then marinade in oil, salt and spices of choice. Bake at 300 for 45-60 min. These will store well for 2 weeks.

DARK CHOCOLATE POPCORN: Heat a pot with a drop or more or oil, add in some dried corn kernels and cover. Shake every couple minutes until all the corn is popped. Mix in coconut flakes and drizzle with dark chocolate (cocoa paste/powder, coconut oil, agave, and vanilla).

SEEDED FRIES: Boil some white or red potatoes and store them in the fridge. Slice them up to make fries along with one sweet potato. Coat with garlic, salt, sesame seeds (white/black) and hemp seeds. Bake in the oven at 350 degrees on parchment paper for at least 1 hour - flip and bake longer if you cut thick.

LOADED MISO SOUP: Simmer mushrooms, Broccoli, Onion, Ginger, Garlic, Water, Organic broth or water, 1 or more heaping teaspoon of miso, Tofu (optional), Carrots/Celery (optional). Garnish with sea veggie flakes, sesame seeds, and green onion.

PESTO PASTA: Add 1/3 cup of cashews, 1/3 cup of coconut oil, 1 head of garlic, and 1/3 cup of nutritional yeast to your food processor and top it off with micro-greens of choice. Simmer the sauce and pour over spaghetti squash, spiralized zucchini or whole rice pasta.

CASHEW PARMESAN: Add 3 tablespoons of nutritional yeast, ¾ cup cashews, garlic and Himalayan sea salt to your food processor. Crumble on your pasta dish.

GARDEN TO GRILL PLATTER: Gather everything from the garden, fridge, and your imagination. Heat up the bbq or light a fire it's grilling time!

>**GRILLED ZUCCHINI:** Slice it, spice it, and coat with some chickpea flour for an extra crispy bite.
>
>**GRILLED MUSHROOMS:** Marinate with balsamic vinegar or liquid aminos and your favorites herbs overnight.
>
>**GRILLED CORN:** Soak whole corn (husk on) in a sink of water for 20 minutes or longer and then grill them. Once cooked through you can remove the husk and add all the flavorings you like.
>
>**GRILLED PEPPERS:** For small peppers, chop off the top and for bigger ones, slice them lengthwise. Stuff them with vegan feta (sprouted almonds, apple cider vinegar, garlic, and salt) or coat them in coconut oil and spices.
>
>**BROCCOLI AND LENTIL BURGERS:** In a food processor, combine 1 cup of sprouted red lentils, 1 cup broccoli, ¼ cup mushrooms, ¼ cup onion, ¼ cup puffed brown rice, 3 tablespoons chia seeds, coriander, cumin, and salt. Create patties and cook them on a cast iron pan with a steel spatula to make sure they stay together.

ASHLEY MICHAUD

GRILLED PINEAPPLE: Slice pineapple and grill. Take it to the next level and add some chipotle seasoning.

FORAGER'S PIE: Cook sprouted green lentils in a vegetable broth. Add in garlic, onion, celery, peas, tomatoes, carrots, thyme, oregano, and Himalayan sea salt. Fill ramekins with this mixture and top with mashed potatoes or cauliflower. Take it a step further and drizzle with natural ketchup. Bake at 350 degrees for 30 minutes.

WELLNESS TINCTURES & REMEDIES

BURDOCK TEA: ½ teaspoon Peppermint Leaves and ½ teaspoon Burdock Root

DANDELION COFFEE: 1 ½ tablespoons of dried dandelion root (less if you are using powder), 2 cups of boiled water, Coconut cream (optional), Natural sweetener (optional), Cinnamon, ginger, vanilla (optional)

POISON IVY REMEDY: Once you harvest your jewelweed let them sweat for a few days or put them into the dehydrator. Add the flowers to a colored glass jar and cover in your favorite carrier oil (almond, olive, sunflower or avacado are great choices). Set this in the window for a couple of weeks to catch the sun and moon light. You can skip this step and apply fresh flowers or take it to the next level and make a cream by straining the flowers and combining the oil with melted beeswax.

ELDERBERRY TINCTURE: Build up your immunity to the cold/flu or relive the if you already have it try our go-to recipe which is tried, true and toddler-friendly. Fill a glass jar with elderberries and cover with apple cider vinegar. Let this sit in the cupboard for 2 weeks or up to 1 year. When you need it to strain the berries and add the tincture to a dropper bottle. Short on elderberry in your area? Echinacea also grows wild this time of year and a great alternative - however, it's not toddler-taste-test friendly.

JUNIPER SPRAY & TONER: Mix 1 tablespoon of juniper berry infused witch hazel, 1 tablespoon aloe vera gel, 3 drops of lavender essential oil.

JUNIPER INFUSED WITCH HAZEL: Fill a dark jar with dried berries. Top with witch hazel and infuse for 1-2 weeks. Pretty Plantain Oil: Fill a Mason Jar with plantain leaves and cover with olive oil. Set this in your window for 2

weeks. Drain your oil through cheesecloth and use as a face serum or mix your infused oil with sea salt and use as a body scrub.

HIKERS' PERFUME: This 2oz bottle of perfume will ward off flies, mosquitos, sand fleas and more… Mix witch hazel, carrier oil of choice, 10-20 drops of lavender essential oil and 10-20 drops of eucalyptus essential oil and top the rest with water.

AFTER BITE: Apply apple cider vinegar to area to reduce the itch and help your bite heal faster. Witch hazel or tea tree oil will also provide immediate relief.

ROSEHIP POWDER CLEANSER: In a blender combine ¼ cup of rolled oats, ¼ cup of bentonite clay, 2 tablespoons of activated charcoal and 1 tablespoon of rosehip oil. Sprinkle on wet hands and rub into face, rinse with warm water and a cloth.

ROSEHIP WATER: Simmer rose clippings in the water on low heat for 1-hour lid on. Remove from heat and strain into a glass jar. Use this as a natural alternative to toner and high priced micellar waters.

ROSEHIP CREAM: Meltdown ¼ cup of coconut oil and 2 tablespoons of beeswax. Remove from heat and add in 1 tablespoon of almond oil, ½ teaspoon of rosehip oil and ¼ teaspoon of lavender essential oil. Lastly, whisk or blend in ¼ cup of aloe vera gel. This cream is good for face, body, kids, sunscreen, and after sun lotion.

Final Thoughts

"A journey of a thousand miles begins with a single step."
– Lao Tzu, Tao Te Ching

While my own Elemental Growth journey continues to evolve, the tools and techniques in this guide book still help me find balance in all areas of my life. I consider it a Farmers' Almanac for the soul and I hope that it helps you turn your passion into action and make your life a masterpiece. In fact, that's probably the biggest takeaway from building this lifestyle: **Life is what you make it. You have the power within you to create the life you desire. Your reality can be exactly what you want, as long as you live with purpose.**

To expand on this thought, everything you do, the thoughts you think, and the places, people, and enviroment you surround yourself with is your decision. What I did differently is this: I started making decisions that benefitted me and aligned myself to nature's patterns in order to eliminate the patterns I manifested that no longer served me.

Talking about change is easy, implementation is the area most people find challenging. Why? Because we live in a culture that expects instant solutions, instant graticification, bandaid cures to patterns and many other ailments and illnesses that take place over the course of several years. We do not give ourselves the grace and patience we need while undergoing a lifestyle change. We need to honor the process over perfection because building and breaking patterns / habits takes time. In the words of Terence McKenna, *"If you don't have a plan, you will fall into someone else's plan,"* and that will suck your life force energy, eventually transforming you into a low-vibrational version of yourself, and believe me when I say this, you have far too much potential to let that happen.

It's true what they say about taking one step forward and two steps back, we have all experienced this once or in some cases, multiple times. The key is accepting that this one-two step dance is part of the growth procress and continue working towards your goals anyway. There is nothing I like more than a true story that expresses just how possible it is to achieve what was once thought to be impossible. It's not going to happen overnight, so take that into account and prepare yourself to notice the signs of an imbalance and have a protocol to get back in the game when you mess up.

Take things one step at time. Think about it like your climbing Mt. Everest—you don't just climb up, you lose something, learn something, hit milestones, and visit base camps as you climb. Some people may have the advantage, but everyone has the opportunity to show up and climb up, so long as they don't give up and continue to pick themselves up no matter how steep the climb or how often they lose their footing. As long as you play the victim in your life, you will always feel like you are missing something you never knew. You will be that lost puzzle piece that doesn't find it's home and continue to shape-shift and change form—losing who you are in the process of neglecting yourself by ignoring what your body and soul have been trying to tell you. Do yourself and the world a favor, and just show-up, even if it's just for today.

When we connect with nature, when we tune into our soul and body, and also connect with others who are showing up, we can reconstruct the world and actively pioneer sociocultural change at a grassroots level. We have been programed to give away our personal power through the generations and when we show up in our life—truly show up—we take that power back. In yoga, I learned the mantra: *"The past is out, the present is in, the future is clear."* This one phrase holds so much power in it because it truly emphasizes how powerful we can be when we no longer allow the past to have a stronghold on us. It allows for a clear mind and heart which then allows us to focus on the present while gaining immense clarity on the future.

Make the decision to be present, to listen to the voices in your head, to lean into that feeling in your gut and notice how your body is eliminating / holding toxins—let that little voice be a big one. Breathe through the negativity and choose to speak to yourself with positivity. Breathe through your fears and feel a sense of safety because the universe is conspiring in your favor, every single time. So choose what lights you up, what keeps you healthy, happy, and whole, and watch how the Universe constantly sends your signs, messengers, and of course abundant opportunities to truly create the life you desire.

My intention in publishing this book is for every single person out there to see that it is absolutely possible to rise up from the rubble, to rebuild your life, to make something of yourself, to live a life that truly fulfills you. I truly believe that we all have a Divine purpose and don't believe in coincidences. It's no coincidence that you are reading this book right now either. The goal now is to loosen up and finally free yourself of all that has held you back so that you rise up, be your best self in body, mind, and soul. Like the tiny seed that knew it had to rise up from the darkness before it could become the evergreen tree, so too can you. Nurture yourself, nourish yourself, and love yourself a little more every single day.

Elemental Growth Index

A

AROMATHERAPY

Aromatherapy uses plant materials and aromatic plant oils, including essential oils, and other aromatic compounds for improving overall well-being.

AMAZON RAINFOREST CONSERVANCY

A registered Canadian Charity actively conserving and preserving land in the Amazon Rainforest which would otherwise be destroyed.

B

BOUNDARIES

Set limits for yourself of what you will and will not allow into your life, then honor them.

C

CHAKRA BALANCING

Using intention, crystals and aromatherapy we can break through any blockages and create a healthy flow of energy.

CLEANSING

A popular method used to help the body heal, recover, and get back to its ideal weight, however, so many people take this route alone and rely on products to support their journey. I make this process fun and support with many tools and techniques that support your health goals while also nourishing your body and quieting your mind.

COACHING

My coaching programs facilitate healthy, sustainable behavior changes by challenging my clients to tap into their inner wisdom, identify their values, and transform their goals into action.

CRYSTAL HEALING

Crystals harness energy & balance the body. For thousands of years, ancient civilizations have used the life giving elements of the earth and the universe.

D

DETOXING

A popular method used to help the body heal, recover and get back to its ideal weight, however, so many people take this route alone and rely on products to support their journey. I make this process fun and support with many tools and techniques that support your health goals while also nourishing your body and quieting your mind.

DISTANCE REIKI

Use this time for yourself or a friend. This creates many beneficial effects in the body, emotions, mind, and spirit.

E

ELEMENTAL GROWTH

Embodying the powers of nature to generate positive growth in all areas of your life.

F

FASTING

A popular method used to help the body heal, recover and get back to its ideal weight, however, so many people take this route alone and rely on products to support their journey. I make this process fun and support with many tools and techniques that support your health goals while also nourishing your body and quieting your mind.

FORWARD THINKING

With an uprising amount of disease and a decreasing quality of life for us and our planet positive change is here. With time comes awareness, with time comes innovation and with time comes healing.

G

GROWTH

The process of increasing in amount, value, or importance.

H

HERBOLOGY

This medical treatment has been used through much of human history. Plants are used in different ways to heal internal/external ailments. This is a holistic approach using nature.

HEALTHMEANS

HealthMeans is providing you with advice from our vast collection of medical experts in order to help you continue moving down your path of health and wellness. Our mission is to bridge the gap between where you are now and where you truly want to be. Our community exists to facilitate your discovery–because you never know when you'll find that one piece of health advice you've truly needed.

I

INDIVIDUALIZED NUTRITION

If you are unsure what foods fuel your body for success, I have many tools that I share with clients to help them uncover their unique and balanced diet, cook strategically, enjoy more plant foods and eat all foods from sustainable and healthy sources.

INTEGRATIVE NUTRITION

True health is about more than simply diet and exercise; it requires balancing all the different aspects of life to nourish your mind, body and spirit. These include relationships, career, healthy food, fun fitness, spirituality, our environment, and more.

INTUITIVE HEALING

Intuitive healing integrates the elements, intuition techniques and senses to locate and correct imbalances in the energy flow within the body.

K

KARMA

Karma therapy guides clients to share their stories in a way that can be captured for their self healing. It also encourages forward thinking, helps uncover your purpose in life & tap into your full potential.

KUNDALINI

Kundalini refers to a form of primal energy said to be located at the base of the spine. In Hindu tradition, Bhairavi is the goddess of Kundalini. Kundalini awakenings may happen through a variety of methods.

M

MOMENTUM

The impetus and driving force gained by the development of a process or course of events.

N

NATURAL ALTERNATIVES

My love for plants and nature is the foundation of Elemental Growth and aligning others with nature is my dharma (purpose in life). Using plants for food & medicine was the answer for me and since your here, maybe for you too. Connecting to nature's messages and tapping into my natural flow as a woman and mother is what continues to drive my own healing journey. To share natures messages with the world, with you, that is the greatest gift I have received.

NATURE

Nature is used as a treatment for behavior modification and self-improvement, by aligning yourself to nature and spending time in it you will naturally heal, reboot and align with your authenticity.

O

ONNIT

Onnit inspires peak performance through a combination of unique products and actionable information. Combining bleeding-edge science, earth-grown nutrients, and time-tested strategies from top athletes and medical professionals, we are dedicated to providing our customers with supplements, foods, and fitness equipment aimed at helping people achieve a new level of well-being we call Total Human Optimization.

P

PERSONAL GROWTH

Life is its own education. Personal development improves awareness and identity, develops talents and potential, enhances the quality of life, and allows you to live your passions and dreams.

R

REIKI MASTER MENTORSHIP

Reiki gives us the ability to heal ourselves and others. Our potential as we practice channeling our natural energy is unlimited and creates opportunities for Elemental Growth. Those who choose to pursue the path of Reiki are not only receiving a gift to heal as a career, but also receiving the powers to heal all life including our animals, soils, planet energy. Those who have been initiated into Reiki often aspire to continue on to the Master levels.

REIKI TEACHINGS

Although becoming a true master is a continuous and lifelong process, my Reiki Teacher Training is the first step to starting your own practice and teaching others the magic of Reiki healing therapies. There are three levels to complete before becoming a master. Training with me, we will cover each of degree of Reiki and I will guide you to start practicing right away.

REIKI THERAPY

Reiki is a relaxation and energetic healing therapy. As a Reiki Master, I have been trained to recognize when a chakra is blocked or out of balance. Chakras draw in energy and govern your hormones, organs and glands. When your chakras are in harmony you become happier, healthier and more attuned to yourself. Your mind alone cannot nurture your entire being and neither can a proper food diet solve all of your health problems. It is by aligning with your natural energy (the unique energy that you were born with) that you can create balance and bring harmony to your mind, body, and spirit.

S

SEASONS

Each of the four divisions of the year (spring, summer, autumn, and winter) are marked by particular weather patterns and daylight hours, resulting from the earth's changing position with regard to the sun.

SELF-LOVE

Self-love is a way of relating to yourself that does not involve harshly judging or punishing yourself for every mistake you make but instead honors the process of progress as well as compassion & forgiveness.

SPIRITUAL BIZ

As a part of my coaching and Reiki Master Mentorship I offer Spiritual Biz Coaching, this includes a rotation of coaching circles as well as guidance from me as you sink into your new role as a spiritual entrepreneur.

SUPERFOOD

Superfood is a hot topic in the health food world. They are most usually plant-based foods that show increased health benefits as a result of its nutritional analysis or its overall nutrient density. I guide my clients on how to purchase, grow, forage or use superfoods in your diet to heal your body, increase energy and balance hormones.

T

THE INSTITUTE OF INTEGRATIVE NUTRITION

This is where I learned over 100 dietary theories, life coaching, and received special training from the top experts in Health & Wellness from around the world. I decided to carry on my education with IIN after graduation to become an expert in Hormone Health, Writing, Publishing, and Business. Aside from my credentials and continuous learning, to me, Integrative Nutrition has always been about connection and community.

THERAPIES

Browse the healing techniques that I integrate into my coaching programs. Elemental Therapies cleanse, balance and activate natural healing, this restores physical/emotional well-being.

TRADITIONAL REIKI

Harmonize and promote the health of body, mind and spirit. Reiki unify's and enhances the natural healing process

W

WILD FOOD

I teach and coach my clients all about how you can include more wild foods and herbs into your diet to nourish your body, mind, align with nature, use quality ingredients and save money on your grocery bill.

Y

YOGA

A Hindu spiritual and ascetic discipline, a part of which, including breath control, simple meditation, and the adoption of specific bodily postures, is widely practiced for health and relaxation.

Acknowledgment

First, I want to thank you, my readers for getting involved in the creation of this book and for taking your life into your own hands. It's all happening!

This book was inspired by my experience at the Institute for Integrative Nutrition® (IIN), where I received my training in holistic wellness, nutrition, and health coaching. Pursuing my education at IIN truly was a life changing experience. It helped me reach optimal health and balance. From the physical aspects of nutrition and eating wholesome foods that work best or each individual person, to the concept of primary food – the idea that everything in life, including our spirituality, career, relationships, and fitness contributes to our inner and outer health. IIN helped me reach optimal health and balance. This inner journey unleashed the passion that compels me to share what I've learned and inspire others.

And lastly, I would like to thank every single person who has contributed to this book coming together. Without you, this wouldn't have been possible.

About the Author

Ashley Michaud is a mother to a very spirited and loving three-year-old boy, Fynn, and an author, health coach, Reiki master, and founder of Elemental Growth. Her mission is to inspire and empower you to heal yourself so that we can can heal our earth as an empowered collective.

HOW ELEMENTAL GROWTH CAME TO BE

Ashley has always found different ways to express herself through art, food, holistic practice, and most recently, writing. With all the resources and new ways to connect with like-minded people that are now available, Ashley was instantly drawn to the idea of starting her own blog.

    While studying at the Institute for Integrative Nutrition, she developed four seasonal groups with an intent to guide others to embrace change through nature, food, love, and movement. It felt so good to birth these season coaching programs that Ashley eventually rebranded as Elemental Growth — a company known today for our inspiration, health tips, natural recipes, and unique style of coaching.

SOME FUN FACTS ABOUT ASHLEY

- She is a single mother to a very happy and healthy toddler named Fynn.
- She is most passionate about personal growth and using plants as food & medicine.
- She is an advocate for plant freedoms, conscious expanding fungi & others.
- She mainly consumes a plant-based diet which excludes many toxins found in the SAD diet today.
- She has lived in four Canadian provinces and the state of New York.
- She has traveled to three countries in South America and cannot wait to go back.
- Ashley's big-audacious-vivacious personal dream is to own a homestead that seconds as an Airbnb where I can model permaculture and an eco-style lifestyle.
- The craziest thing on Ashley's bucket list is holding a retreat on each of the planets energy centers - The first retreat will be held in the Shasta Mountains in California.

PHILANTHROPY

Aside from how Ashley takes action in her own life and business, she is also on the board of directors for The

Be The Change

Amazon Rainforest Conservancy. ARC is saving threatened tropical Rainforest habitats in the Peruvian jungle acre by acre. Currently they have 1,416 hectares (3,500 acres) of land in their care, which the team is passionate about preserving and conserving to protect the biodiversity and enhance the survival of wildlife, species and ecosystems.

Your donation will help us continue to purchase threatened tropical Rainforest habitats in Tambopata, Peru for conservation, protection, education and research.

WHY YOU SHOULD CARE

- Global market forces threaten the very existence of the Amazon Rainforest, despite scientists having determined it plays a key role in the basic functioning of the planet.
- Preventing deforestation helps mitigate climate change, which affects the health and well being of families and economies throughout the world. Peru does not have the financial means to curb destruction to its Rainforest.

HOW YOU CAN SUPPORT US

Your donation (big/small) allows ARC to conserve and protect land that might otherwise be damaged from illegal gold mining, logging, poaching and other activities. We are a volunteer driven charity and all funds received are directed to land conservation work.

DONATE AT

www.amazonrainforestconservancy.com/

Notes

Notes

Notes

Notes

Manufactured by Amazon.ca
Bolton, ON